A HISTORY OF
THE RAILWAYS OF
NORTHAMPTONSHIRE

'Royal Scot' 4-6-0 No 6147 *The Northamptonshire Regiment* at Crewe in August 1935. Two plaques were to be fitted over the nameplates after a ceremony in Northampton in October of that year. *Stapleton/Butler collection*

A History of the Railways of

Northamptonshire

Peter Butler

MOTOR CAR ACTS, 1896 AND 1903.

NOTICE.

THIS BRIDGE IS INSUFFICIENT TO CARRY A HEAVY MOTOR CAR THE REGISTERED AXLE WEIGHT OF ANY AXLE OF WHICH EXCEEDS THREE TONS, OR THE REGISTERED AXLE WEIGHTS OF THE SEVERAL AXLES OF WHICH EXCEED IN THE AGGREGATE FIVE TONS, OR A HEAVY MOTOR CAR DRAWING A TRAILER IF THE REGISTERED AXLE WEIGHTS OF THE SEVERAL AXLES OF THE HEAVY MOTOR CAR AND THE AXLE WEIGHTS OF THE SEVERAL AXLES OF THE TRAILER EXCEED IN THE AGGREGATE FIVE TONS.

EAST AND WEST JUNCTION, STRATFORD-ON-AVON, TOWCESTER AND MIDLAND JUNCTION RAILWAYS. STRATFORD-ON-AVON.

· RAILWAY HERITAGE ·
from
The NOSTALGIA Collection

This book is dedicated to the late
Fred Cockman
of Bedford, a dear friend and a real railway historian

First published in 2006

British Library Cataloguing in Publication Data

A catalogue record for this book is available from the British Library.

ISBN 1 85794 281 7
ISBN 978 1 85794 281 1

Silver Link Publishing Ltd
The Trundle
Ringstead Road
Great Addington
Kettering
Northants NN14 4BW

Tel/Fax: 01536 330588
email: sales@nostalgiacollection.com
Website: www.nostalgiacollection.com

Printed and bound in Great Britain

Half title Back in familiar territory, preserved 'Jubilee' No 5690 *Leander* passes northbound through Wellingborough on a special on 8 April 2006. *Author*

Title page A E&WJR/ST&MJR bridge plate from Wappenham – something for the Plain English Society to get to grips with! *F. G. Cockman*

ACKNOWLEDGEMENTS

Over the years many people have provided me with help and information for this book. It would be impossible to name everyone involved, but I must mention some: Robert Wharton for his encouragement, Will Adams for his involvement and interest, Barry Taylor and Geoffrey Starmer for helping with information, Richard Casserley for granting me access to his and his late father's photographic collection, my long-suffering wife Lilian for trying to keep me on the grammatical track, and finally, but not least, John Downing of Northampton, my constant companion over many years as we have wandered all over the county tracing the railways of yesteryear. To everyone who has helped in any way, my sincere thanks.

CONTENTS

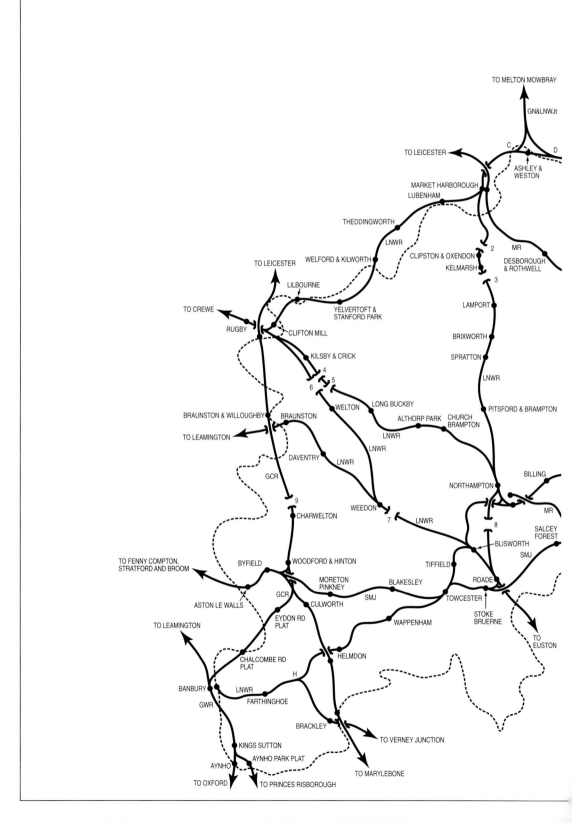

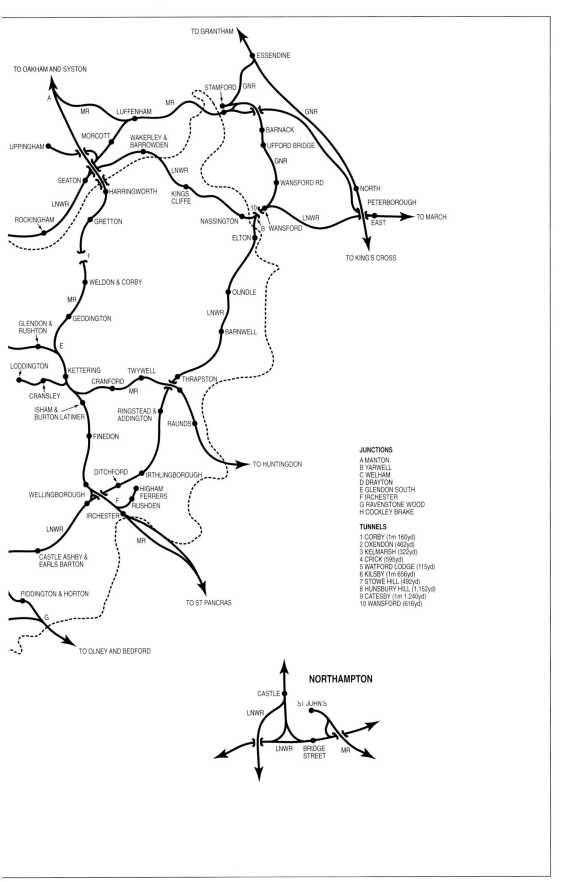

Fifty-five years of progress on Northamptonshire's railways: the famous pioneering diesel-electric twins Nos 10000 and 10001 pass the north end of the Gayton Loops on the West Coast Main Line with the up 'Royal Scot' in July 1950, and a modern-day view of Wellingborough (Midland Road) station with a 'Meridian' four-car set on a down service in March 2005. *Les Hanson/Author*

INTRODUCTION

Anyone attempting to learn something of the railways in Northamptonshire will find that it is necessary to refer to a large selection of material in order to get a complete picture.

For some time now I have felt that there was need for a book that would cover the railways of the county, not at an in–depth level, but sufficient to give the readers an adequate picture of why and how they were built, and one which, if accompanied with a good Bibliography, would enable them to further their studies.

One of the first decisions that had to be made was to establish what determined the county? Over the years the boundaries have changed; for example, in 1974 the Soke of Peterborough became part of Cambridgeshire. For this study it was decided to use the boundaries that exist today, but to sometimes stray outside for the sake of completeness.

At one time there were more than 70 stations in the county. Today there are only five, at Kings Sutton, Long Buckby, Northampton, Kettering and Wellingborough. Over the last few years the sites of all the stations have been visited to see what, if anything, remains of a system of lines that ranged from the three key routes that radiated out from London and spread on a north/south axis through the county, to the humble branch lines that meandered through the countryside.

Mention will be made throughout the book of various sites of interest that were still in place in recent years. Having said that, it should be emphasised that nothing remains static. Some sites survived for decades almost untouched, yet on a further visit only months later were found to be devoid of any signs at all. It must also be stressed that where buildings remain they are in private hands and permission should be sought either to visit or photograph them.

Thankfully the county boasts some excellent examples of the skill and expertise of the early railway civil engineers, the deep cutting at Roade, the rail overbridge at Blisworth and the splendid 82-arch viaduct at Harringworth being good examples that are still used by rail traffic today.

After some thought it was decided not to cover the complex rail networks that evolved with the iron-ore quarrying that took place over large areas of the county. The late Eric Tonks made this his lifelong study, and his books on the subject, written in great depth and clarity, are likely to remain the definitive works for the foreseeable future. However, reference will be made to them, for example in the case of the Stratford-upon-Avon & Midland Junction Railway, which was built principally for the transport of iron ore. Additionally, the decision was made not to cover details of the various locomotives that worked over the county's rail network; this again has been well documented in the past.

With any work of this nature, there will be mistakes, and for these I accept full responsibility.

FURTHER READING

Books are listed in the order in which the lines they deal with appear in the book.

British Railway History (2 vols) C. Hamilton Ellis (Allen & Unwin, 1954 & 1959)

Canals of the East Midlands Charles Hadfield (David & Charles, 1966)

Rails over Blisworth Hill Victor Hatley (Northampton Historical Series No 2, 1970)

London & Birmingham Railway David Gould (David & Charles, 1987)

London & Birmingham David Jenkinson (Capital Transport Publishing, 1988)

Weedon and its Depot John Wagstaff (Author, 1994)

The Nene Valley Railway John Rhodes (Turntable Publications, 1983)

British Railways Past and Present Companion: The Nene Valley Railway Christopher Awdry (Past & Present, 2001)

Northampton and Harborough Line John Gough (Railway & Canal Historical Society, 1984)

The London & North Western Railway O. S. Nock (Ian Allan, 1960)

Track Diagrams of the London & North Western Railway and its Successors (Section 5 Northamptonshire) R. D. Foster and M. R. L. Instone (Wild Swan, 1988)

The Stratford-upon-Avon & Midland Junction Railway J. M. Dunn (Oakwood Press, 1952)

The Stratford-upon-Avon & Midland Junction Railway Arthur Jordan (Oxford Railway Publishing Co, 1982)

The Stratford-upon-Avon & Midland Junction Railway R. C. Riley & Bill Simpson (Lamplight Publications, 1999)

Williams's Midland Railway: It's rise and progress F. S. Williams (1876, David & Charles 1968)

Midland Chronology John Gough (Railway & Canal Historical Society, 1989)

The Kettering-Huntingdon Line John Rhodes (Oakwood Press, 1984)

Life and Work among the Navvies (Kettering-Manton line) Rev D. W. Barrett (1879, Silver Link 2003)

The Rushden-Higham Ferrers Branch P. E. B. Butler (Author, 1994)

Woodford Halse: A railway community Ruth Irons & Stanley Jenkins (Oakwood Press, 1999)

The Last Years of the Great Central Main Line R. Robotham (Ian Allan, 1986)

History of the Railways of Oxfordshire Part 1 Bill Simpson (Lamplight Publications, 1997)

Railways of Buckinghamshire F. G. Cockman (*Records of Buckinghamshire* Vol XIX Part 2, 1972)

The GWR & GCR Joint Railway S. C. Jenkins (Oakwood Press, 1978)

Blakesley Hall Railway P. B. Kingston (Dr Bob Tebb, Ravenglass, 2003)

Wicksteeds Park Railway D. Nelson (Wicksteeds Park, 2006)

The Railways of Northamptonshire 1800-1960 C. R. Clinker (Author, 1960)

Opening and Closing of Public Railway Stations (2nd ed) M. E. Quick (Railway & Canal Historical Society, 2003)

The Age of the Electric Train J. C. Gillham (Ian Allan, 1988)

Regional History of the Railways of Great Britain: East Midlands R. Leleux (David & Charles, 1976 & 1984)

Forgotten Railways: Chiltern & Cotswolds Davies & Grant (David & Charles, 1984)

Victorian Transport Schemes 1863-1900 Gerald Mann (Newton Business Solutions, Litchborough, 1996)

Journals of the Northants Natural History Society

The Railway Magazine

Railway World

Trains Illustrated

Research Papers of G. N. Webb, F. G. Cockman and G. Starmer

Various timetables

BLISWORTH HILL RAILWAY

Ask anyone which was the first railway in the county and I suspect many would say the London & Birmingham. However, to give as complete a picture as possible, we must start with what became known as 'The Blisworth Hill Tramway'.

The Grand Junction Canal, authorised by an Act of Parliament in 1793, was built to link the River Thames at Brentford in Middlesex with the Oxford Canal at Braunston in Northamptonshire. William Praed, a banker, was one of the promoters and would eventually become the Chairman. Also on the board was the Duke of Grafton, a gentleman who was to become very much involved with the canal and tramway in the county; we will encounter him again as we look at the history of the London & Birmingham Railway. William Jessop was appointed as the consultant engineer, while James Barnes became the resident engineer.

It was realised from the start that the biggest problem would be driving the canal through the Northamptonshire uplands. The only practical way would be by means of tunnels, one at Braunston, shortly before the canal met the Oxford Canal, and a second that would link Blisworth and Stoke Bruerne. Work started at both ends of the canal and also on the two tunnels. Although it was the second tunnel that was to give the builders so much trouble, the one at Braunston had its problems, not least being a miscalculation with the surveying, with the result that the tunnel ended up with a bit of a bend in it.

By 1796 the canal had reached Blisworth from the north, but work on the tunnel there was running into trouble. There were various factors at play, but the principal problem was flooding, which may seem strange for a canal tunnel. The following year, 1797, work on the tunnel was abandoned, and the company decided to concentrate on the completion of the rest of the canal while working out how best to tackle the problem. One of the ideas was to build a series of locks over the hill, but Barnes felt that the answer was still to have a tunnel, but to use a different route from the original. A great deal of discussion must have taken place because work did not restart until 1802. Meanwhile, in 1800 the canal had reached Stoke Bruerne from the south.

During the intervening period the company had no choice but to tranship freight from barges on to wagons and haul them over Blisworth Hill, and do the same operation in reverse at Stoke Bruerne. Initially the company built a toll road over the hill, but with ever-increasing amounts of traffic it was soon realised that a better method of transportation was needed. William Jessop suggested that the answer was to build a 'cast-iron' tramway over Blisworth Hill. Jessop and a Benjamin Outram and others were partners of the Butterley Iron Company in Derbyshire, and although it could be said that they had a vested interest in Jessop's recommendation, nevertheless it was the right answer for the canal company.

The Butterley Company produced cast-

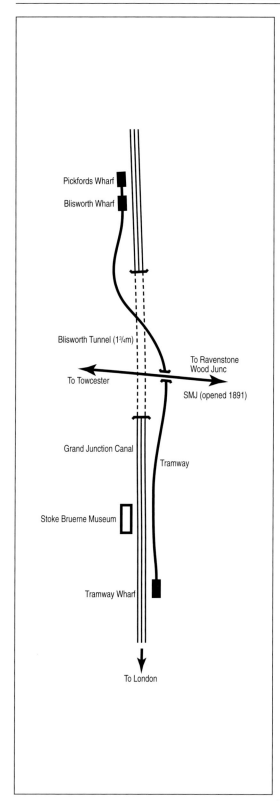

Pickfords Wharf

Blisworth Wharf

Blisworth Tunnel (1¾m)

To Ravenstone
Wood Junc

To Towcester

SMJ (opened 1891)

Grand Junction Canal

Tramway

Stoke Bruerne Museum

Tramway Wharf

To London

Blisworth Hill Railway, opened by January 1801.

iron rails with an L-shaped configuration, which were usually between 3 and 4 feet long. The joints were supported by square stone blocks. Unlike conventional railways, where the flange is on the wheel, with this system the flange was on the rail. The beauty of this system was that, providing the wheels on the wagon or cart were the right gauge, they could easily be rolled on to the tramway and just as easily off and back on to the road. Between the rails a hard surface was provided, to make it easier for the horse or horses pulling the load.

One of the biggest landowners in this part of the county at that time was the aforementioned Duke of Grafton. He seems to have been the sort of person whose first reaction, when faced with something new, says no, then goes away and thinks about it and comes to the realisation that perhaps this new idea has potential from which he could benefit.

When first faced with the tramway coming over his land he was opposed to it, fearing that it would upset his tenants and perhaps his hunting. However, the Act for the Canal of 1793 included the right to compulsorily buy land, so didn't pursue his opposition. Since he was on the board of the canal company it was important to him that the canal was completed as soon as possible so that its potential – and of course its profitability – could be fully realised.

In June 1799 the board agreed to the building of the tramway over Blisworth Hill and work commenced soon afterwards. The main part of the double-track line was open towards the end of 1800, and a small stretch northwards at Blisworth was added at the beginning of the following year. It continued in use until March 1805, when, at last, the tunnel was completed.

These days we are all being urged to

recycle as many things as possible, so it is interesting to note, when we see what happened next, that this practice was already in use in 1805. The inhabitants of Northampton were complaining that they were being missed out by the canals, and all the benefits they could bring, so the Grand Junction agreed to build a branch from its canal at Gayton Wharf to South Bridge in Northampton, where it would make a connection with the River Nene. While this was being done, the company used many of the rails, etc, from the by now redundant tramroad at Blisworth to provide a double set of rails to Northampton. This opened in October 1805 and was to remain in use until the branch canal opened in May 1815. It is interesting to note that this second tramway was longer, both in distance and length of

Blisworth canal tunnel exhaust in February 2003 (*right*), a plain affair compared with the more grandiose exhaust of the L&B's Kilsby Tunnel, photographed in April 1995. *Both author*

Seen from the trackbed of the Blisworth Hill Railway near Stoke Bruerne in February 2003, the bridge abutments are those of the Easton Neston Mineral & Towcester Roade & Olney Junction Railway section of the SMJ. *Author*

time in service, than the original Blisworth Hill Tramway, and would therefore have needed new materials to complete the line.

Little did they know it, but before long many of these same inhabitants of Northampton would be clamouring for their own railway. The rapid growth of the railway system throughout the country in the coming years would see the decline of the canal system as a bulk carrier of goods. Today, with only a very small amount of goods travelling

by canal, it is the leisure industry that has kept them open, and even for old stretches of canal to be brought back into service. Now, at the start of the 21st century, there are plans for new canals to be built, including one from the Grand Union at Milton Keynes to the River Ouse at Bedford. (The Grand Junction Canal became part of the Grand Union Canal in 1929.)

Today it is possible to walk most of the route of the original tramway, and it was while doing this in 2003 that I noticed a piece of metal sticking up from beneath a hedge. It turned out to be a piece of rail from the tramway, which was subsequently 'rescued'.

LONDON & BIRMINGHAM RAILWAY

The London & Birmingham Railway (L&B), as its name suggests, was built to provide a railway connecting the capital with the country's second city, and from there to the industrial centres of the North West. The opening of the Liverpool & Manchester Railway in 1830, followed by the Grand Junction Railway (Birmingham to Warrington) in July 1837, spurred the promoters to get the L&B under way.

Prior to this there had been plans for lines linking London with the principal industrial centres of England, one of which would have passed through Northampton. Although these plans did not materialise, the feeling was that railways were here to stay and fresh plans were formulated.

Perhaps this might be a good point to stress that by now the canal network had linked most major cities, and the coming of railways was threatening the canal owners' livelihoods, and of course those who operated road coaches.

Two rival companies were established, each favouring a different route between London and Birmingham, the first via Oxford and Banbury, the other via Bletchley, Rugby and Coventry. The former was proposed by Sir John Rennie, the canal builder, and he would obviously have had great experience in surveying routes that kept to fairly level ground. The other proposer was Francis Giles. In 1829 the companies' proposals and surveys were published, and a year later, in September 1830, they decided to amalgamate. The great

George Stephenson and his son Robert, by now well established as railway surveyors and engineers, were to be responsible for the construction of the line, but George soon handed over the work to his son. Robert started work by doing another survey of the two routes, much to the annoyance of both Giles and Rennie, who were now in the same camp! Francis Giles, in particular, had every reason to be annoyed, because when Robert Stephenson revealed the details of his preferred route, it was, to a great extent, the same that Giles had proposed earlier.

Despite earlier hopes that the line would pass through Northampton, it kept to the higher ground to the west and was routed via Blisworth and Weedon. It is true there was opposition from the landed gentry around Northampton and, initially, from the Town Council, but in fairness to the ordinary townsfolk, we know that they were keen from the outset. It is also true that Robert Stephenson said it was easy to get his trains into the town, but it would be more difficult to get them out. It needs to be borne in mind that the line was to connect London and Birmingham, and other places en route would be of secondary importance.

Also, one should not forget the importance of Weedon Barracks to the new line, a fact that the Government would have noted. The Barracks had been built in 1803 at a time when there was a genuine fear that Napoleon might invade England. Its location had been chosen so that it would be in a central

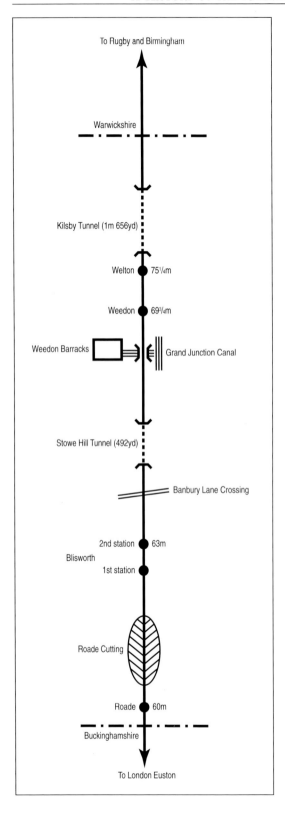

To Rugby and Birmingham

Warwickshire

Kilsby Tunnel (1m 656yd)

Welton ● 75¼m

Weedon ● 69¾m

Weedon Barracks → |€| ⇐ Grand Junction Canal

Stowe Hill Tunnel (492yd)

Banbury Lane Crossing

2nd station ● 63m

Blisworth

1st station ●

Roade Cutting

Roade ● 60m

Buckinghamshire

To London Euston

position in the country as regards roads and canals and would be a long way from the South Coast. Weedon was to become an important storage site for arms and ammunitions and, if necessary, a refuge for King George III.

On 6 May 1833 the L&B had its Act passed by Parliament for a railway from Chalk Farm in London to Curzon Street in Birmingham. Just over a year later another Act sanctioned the extension of the line from Chalk Farm to Euston. Work began in earnest and was to become one of the great engineering feats of its time, with up to 20,000 navvies engaged on it during the four years of its construction.

Northampton, then, missed the main line, just as it had in the canal age, and would have to wait until 1845, with the opening of the Peterborough branch, and 1881, when the loop line opened from Rugby. Over the years it gained a reputation as the town that didn't want a railway. Two of the town's leading historians, Miss Joan Wake and Mr Victor Hatley, fiercely proud of their town, wrote at length in later years in order to vindicate the town and to attempt to prove that the slur on Northampton was unjustified

Construction of the line continued apace. By keeping to the higher ground, Robert Stephenson ran into an unforeseen problem. Despite careful surveying, when construction of the tunnel at Kilsby commenced there was severe flooding. At one time there were plans to re-route the line, just as there had been some 36 years earlier, when similar problems had occurred with the construction of the canal tunnel at Blisworth. In the end it was decided to battle on until all the water that lay in the ground above the tunnel had been drained, or was at least controllable. Some idea of the scale of the problem facing the navvies can be appreciated from the fact that water was being pumped from the tunnel at the rate

London & Birmingham Railway, opened throughout in September 1838 (distances from London Euston).

Welton station looking north in July 1959: note the staggered platforms, with the down platform on the far side of the bridge. *H. C. Casserley*

of 2,000 gallons every minute for months on end!

Another major problem was the cutting at Roade. This is 1½ miles long and up to 65 feet deep, and it must be remembered that the work on it, and the tunnel, was done by hand. Mechanical aids were many decades away; the only help the navvies had was gunpowder, with all the dangers its use involved.

Work was proceeding well on the rest of the line, and it was ready to carry traffic before the tunnel was complete. So, as with the canal earlier, it was decided to open the line and to use stage-coaches to bridge the 36-mile gap between Denbigh Hall (Bucks) and Rugby; a temporary station and hotel were opened at Denbigh Hall until the line was fully open. Eventually, on 17 September 1838, through trains started to run between London and Birmingham. When the line was fully opened there were stations in the county at Roade, Blisworth, Weedon and Crick, though this latter station was to change its name to Welton in 1881. Welton station was somewhat different in that it had staggered platforms.

Roade station opened slightly earlier than the other stations, on 2 July 1838, for the benefit of passengers from Northampton. Sadly, none of these first four stations in the county have survived: Welton closed on 7 July 1958, Weedon on 15 September 1958,

Blisworth (the second station on the site) on 4 January 1960, and Roade on 7 September 1964.

Blisworth had two stations, the first only having a short life. Opened in 1838, it closed at the time of the Peterborough branch opening in 1845. In the September 1904 issue of the *Journal of the Northants Natural History Society* there was a photograph of what was claimed to be Blisworth's first station. The late George Freeston, Blisworth's historian par excellence, to whom I am greatly indebted, kindly told me what the building actually was. The Duke of Grafton, who we first met in the previous chapter, had opened a stone quarry close to the canal at Blisworth. By now he could see that the railways, whether he liked it or not, were becoming a fact of life. He decided to have a pair of villas built close to the railway, which would enable the travelling public to see what splendid stone was available from his quarry. The northern villa was called Ford Villa, and the southern Grafton Villa, and into this villa moved the first Station Master of Blisworth, a Mr Cornelius Flower, his wife and family. This, I suspect is where the mistake was first made; it is not the first station that is referred to in the photograph, but the first Station Master's house.

Most historians in the past have said that

Above The Duke of Grafton's villas at Blisworth in March 2000: the southern one, 'Grafton Villa', was the home of Blisworth's first Station Master. The station was at the top of the embankment behind the villas, and the famous stone overbridge can be seen on the right. *Author*

Below Blisworth's second station in 1953, with Class 5 No 45034 on an up Northampton-Euston train. *R. M. Casserley*

the station was situated to the south of the railway bridge spanning the road into Blisworth. With new railways appearing on the map, it was quite fashionable to provide the travelling public with guides so they could appreciate not only where they were but also learn something of the countryside through which they were travelling. Two such guides were published, the first in 1839 by Thomas Roscoe and the second a year later by W. Osbourne. Roscoe, describing the line between London and Birmingham, writes, '…at a short distance we pass over a lofty bridge of one arch … at this point is a covered staircase leading from the railway (on the embankment) to Blisworth station, which is the 2nd class temporary building…' A modern large-scale OS map of the area shows how the embankment widens out behind the two villas, ie to the north of the bridge, and I am convinced that the station was where Roscoe said it was, namely above the Station Master's house. Of one thing we can be sure – it had a short life, as we shall see when we look at the Peterborough branch. These two houses still stand today at the junction of the main road into Blisworth with Station Road, as does that 'lofty bridge of one arch'.

George Freeston, in his researches into Blisworth's history, also discovered that Richard Dunkley, a local builder, had got involved with either the completion of this bridge, or had been asked to correct some of the faulty workmanship done by the original contractor. What to Dunkley may have been just a one-off job was, in fact, to bring him a great deal more work for the L&B and its successor, the London & North Western Railway (LNWR). He was awarded the contract for the second station at Blisworth together with the adjacent hotel, and he went on to build many of the workshops and workers' houses at Wolverton for the LNWR as well as a great deal of railway building work in the London area.

Increasing traffic levels meant that the LNWR had little or no alternative but to seek Parliamentary permission to quadruple the line between Rugby and London. This was granted in 1875, and the new lines, which went through Northampton, opened in 1881.

All the different railway companies that operated throughout the country were merged into four large companies in 1923. The 'Grouping', as it became known, made little difference to the old LNWR's major trunk route, and neither did nationalisation of the railways in 1948. Two years after nationalisation the timetables just referred to 'Passenger Services – London Midland Region'. It is worth noting that despite 25 years having elapsed between the Grouping and nationalisation, railwaymen still associated themselves with the different pre-Grouping companies, and such friendly rivalry can still be heard today.

In March 1955 the Ministry of Transport announced the electrification of the West Coast Main Line (WCML) from London to Glasgow. The original design was for the electrification to be an overhead system at 1500v DC, but within a year this had been replaced by an overhead system that operated at 25KV AC. This was a most radical step, especially when one considers the mileage involved for a new and untried system. Apart from the inevitable 'blips' in the early days, the system worked well and continues to do so to the present day. The work was done in stages, with the section from Rugby to London being completed as one section, which opened throughout in November 1965. The early 1960s saw a mixture of trains running through the county while the electrification work was being carried out, ranging from traditional steam and diesel locomotive-hauled trains to DMUs. With electrification came new locomotives, rolling-stock and signalling; steam motive power was being phased out and had gone completely by August 1968.

The famous Banbury Lane crossing box in pre-electrification days. *Author's collection*

The crossing today, with an up Virgin 'Pendolino', photographed from the newly opened road overbridge in June 2000. *Author*

One survivor of the old days managed to survive until March 1988. This was the little level crossing gate box at Banbury Lane. I was fortunate to be allowed to visit this box just days before it closed and see how the signalman/gateman coped with high-speed trains yet needing to keep the road barriers down for as short a time as possible. Eventually the crossing was replaced by a flyover in April 2005.

In 1990 Intercity announced an £800 million upgrade of the WCML to enable the introduction of a new generation of trains capable of running at 155mph. In 1992 the privatisation of the railways was proposed by the ruling Conservative Party, and as time

passed their desire to break up and sell the railways increased. By 1995 the entire network had been broken up into 113 parts and sold off, thus bringing to an end 49 years of nationalised railways. The upgrade of the WCML continued under the now defunct privatised company, Railtrack. It is interesting that this part of the railway system, now renamed Network Rail, has effectively been re-nationalised by the ruling Labour Party, following several tragic accidents.

The principal WCML passenger services are now run by Virgin Trains, which is bringing in new trains capable of yet higher speeds, though these are unlikely to benefit Northamptonshire's travellers.

PETERBOROUGH BRANCH

In 1842, four years after the London & Birmingham Railway (L&B) opened its line through the county, and in so doing missed Northampton, a delegation from the town approached the Board of the L&B with a proposal to build a branch line to Peterborough via Northampton. At this time Peterborough still had no railway, although various schemes were being proposed. If the L&B could get there first, not only would Northampton get its railway, but the line would also open up new potential traffic flows that could only be to the benefit of the L&B and the general public. After careful consideration, therefore, the L&B decided to proceed with the line and duly applied to Parliament. Very quickly the local landowners organised petitions against the proposal, just as they had done with the main line. However, their efforts were in vain, and the new line received the Royal Assent on 4 July 1843. Work started in March 1844, with Robert Stephenson again in charge.

Unlike the construction of the L&B main line, with all its difficulties, once the line reached Northampton all that was proposed was to follow the River Nene to Peterborough. The only obstacle was a small hill to the west of Wansford, which would need to be tunnelled through. All roads crossed would be on the level, and a station provided at every place where a turnpike road crossed the line. This would, initially, reduce construction costs considerably, but would increase operating costs, which, in later years,

would be one of the reasons given for justifying closure.

Because the Nene Valley was prone to flooding, much of the track was laid on small embankments, which it was hoped would prevent the line from being flooded. For most of the time this worked, but there were occasions when it disappeared under the waters, as for example in November 1852, when severe flooding swept away several bridges and the line was closed for a week. In total there were 26 level crossings along the branch, 13 bridges over the Nene and the tunnel at Wansford.

Although only a few years had elapsed since the main line had opened, there appear to have been no worries as to whether the locomotives could haul their trains from Northampton to Blisworth, where the branch would start. Had locomotive designs improved so much in so short a space of time?

Meanwhile, to the east of Peterborough the Eastern Counties Railway (ECR) was building a branch from Ely to Peterborough. It was suggested that the L&B and the ECR build a joint station at Peterborough where the two lines would meet; however, this came to nothing and the station was built by the ECR and used by the L&B. To reach this station the L&B had to cross a meadow owned by the Cathedral authorities, which was hired out for fairs, etc, and a charge made for the privilege. The railway would cut the meadow in two, and probably also the Cathedral's takings! The L&B and the ECR

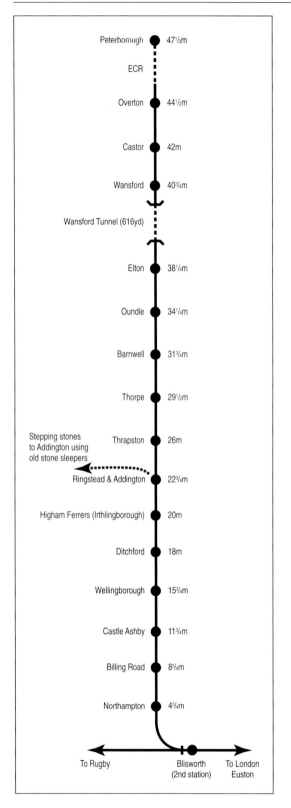

Station	Mileage
Peterborough	47½m
ECR	
Overton	44½m
Castor	42m
Wansford	40¾m
Wansford Tunnel (616yd)	
Elton	38¼m
Oundle	34¼m
Barnwell	31¾m
Thorpe	29½m
Thrapston	26m
Ringstead & Addington	22¾m
Higham Ferrers (Irthlingborough)	20m
Ditchford	18m
Wellingborough	15¾m
Castle Ashby	11¾m
Billing Road	8¾m
Northampton	4¾m

Stepping stones to Addington using old stone sleepers

To Rugby — Blisworth (2nd station) — To London Euston

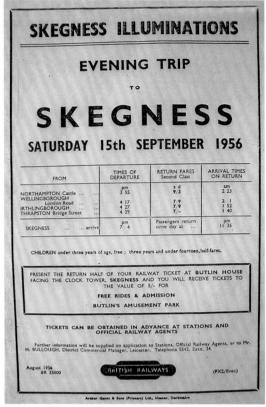

SKEGNESS ILLUMINATIONS

EVENING TRIP

TO

SKEGNESS

SATURDAY 15th SEPTEMBER 1956

FROM	TIMES OF DEPARTURE	RETURN FARES Second Class	ARRIVAL TIMES ON RETURN
	pm	s d	am
NORTHAMPTON Castle	3 55	9/3	2 23
WELLINGBOROUGH London Road	4 17	7/9	2 1
IRTHLINGBOROUGH	4 27	7/9	1 52
THRAPSTON Bridge Street	4 39	7/–	1 40
	pm	Passengers return	pm
SKEGNESS ... arrive	7 4	same day at ...	11 35

CHILDREN under three years of age, free ; three years and under fourteen, half-fares.

PRESENT THE RETURN HALF OF YOUR RAILWAY TICKET AT BUTLIN HOUSE FACING THE CLOCK TOWER, SKEGNESS AND YOU WILL RECEIVE TICKETS TO THE VALUE OF 5/- FOR

FREE RIDES & ADMISSION

BUTLIN'S AMUSEMENT PARK

TICKETS CAN BE OBTAINED IN ADVANCE AT STATIONS AND OFFICIAL RAILWAY AGENTS

Further information will be supplied on application to Stations, Official Railway Agents, or to Mr. H. BULLOUGH, District Commercial Manager, Leicester. Telephone 5542, Extn. 34.

August 1956
BR 35000

BRITISH RAILWAYS

(PX2/Evex)

Arthur Gaunt & Sons (Printers) Ltd., Hasnor, Derbyshire

Far left **Peterborough branch (L&B), opened throughout in June 1845 (distances from Blisworth).**

Left **Handbill from August 1956.**
Author's collection

Below left **Oil-lamp at Thorpe station, photographed in April 1959.**
R. M. Casserley

Right **A delightful shot of the sole surviving Johnson '1P' Class No 20204 at Peterborough East in May 1937 with a train for Northampton.**
H. C. Casserley

reached an agreement that allowed the L&B to have running powers over the ECR, and this seems to have removed the problems raised by the Church. The ECR laid 600 yards of track to the west of its station, which was sufficient to cross the meadow. The nearest the L&B got to having its own station at Peterborough was a small wooden ticket platform to the west of the ECR station, where trains would stop to allow the staff to check the passengers' tickets.

Work continued quickly and the line was opened in two stages, from Blisworth to Northampton in May 1845, then throughout in June 1845. By this date the ECR had still not reached Peterborough, although it had completed the building of its station and connecting track so the L&B could use it.

At Blisworth it was quickly recognised that the original station was in the wrong place for a junction. In April 1845 the L&B Minutes Book records that '…new station to be built at Gayton at junction of Blisworth and Peterborough line. This will allow dispensing with present inadequate station at Blisworth.' Whether the new station was built in time for the opening of the branch a month later is not known; I suspect that the L&B used the first station for a time before the new one was ready. Another problem that the L&B would

have to face was the fact that the junction from the branch faced south, towards London, so any trains wishing to go to Birmingham would have to reverse at the station. We shall see later how the LNWR got round this problem.

In July 1846 the L&B became one of the principal constituents of the new London & North Western Railway (LNWR). Meanwhile, also in 1846, the Syston and Peterborough line of the Midland Railway (MR) had arrived at Peterborough. To be more accurate, the section from Stamford to Peterborough was complete, but because of Lord Harborough's objection to having the railway on his land at Saxby, this part of the line was isolated until the route was opened throughout in May 1848. In the meantime trains on this section were operated by the LNWR; this was a most unusual case of co-operation, with one company running trains for another and using a third company's station! It was not until January 1847 that the ECR reached its station from the east. Having reached Peterborough, the ECR took over from the LNWR the running of the isolated MR section, and for a short period ran a Stamford-Ely service.

Although the trackbed of the Blisworth to Peterborough line had been built for double track throughout, at the time of opening there was only double track between Blisworth and Northampton, and from there to Peterborough was single track. Progress on the construction of the line was quite fast, the major works being the river bridges and the tunnel at Wansford, where several hundred men were employed. Although only just over 600 yards in length, its construction took a year to complete.

On the single-line section between Northampton and Peterborough there was a passing loop at Thrapston, which was roughly half way between the two towns. The theory was that if there was only one locomotive for each section of line, there would be no collisions. However, this arrangement was very short-lived, even if it was ever actually used, because from the opening of the line the electric telegraph was installed throughout, which meant that trains could be signalled. (It is worth recording that the first locomotive on the branch was to be found at Thrapston,

having been hauled by a team of horses from Weedon.)

So the great day arrived on 2 June 1845, and it is quite amazing to think that the 47-mile branch line had been constructed in just over a year. (Today the building of a few miles of road can still take several years to complete, an example being the recent Rushden bypass.) There were stations at Northampton, Castle Ashby, Wellingborough, Ditchford, Higham Ferrers (later Irthlingborough), Ringstead, Thrapston, Thorpe, Barnwell, Oundle, Wansford and Overton. Billing opened in December 1845, and the LNWR opened two further stations at Elton and Castor in 1846.

Almost within weeks of the opening, the L&B was talking about doubling the line throughout its entire length. One suspects that the traffic generated was greater than the company had anticipated and this was leading to delays on the stretches of single line. Work on doubling was completed by September 1846.

Another unusual feature of this line was that, unlike most, the passenger service started first; goods services did not begin until the

Castle Ashby looking towards Northampton in June 1959: note the modern platform lighting! The goods shed in the distance is now a restaurant. *R. M. Casserley*

end of 1845, and even then the company almost had to be pushed into starting them! Compare this with the Rushden and Higham Ferrers branch, where goods services started in September 1893, while passengers had to wait until May of the following year.

Once the service was under way, one of the main sources of traffic was cattle, and another, of course, was coal, which could now be brought in at lower cost. In later years the iron-ore trade became the main source of revenue on the branch. New quarries, some feeding on to the branch, produced the ore for new blast furnaces that were built in Wellingborough, Kettering and Corby. One quarry should be more accurately described as a mine, burrowing between Irthlingborough and Finedon, with a connection being made to the branch between Irthlingborough and Ditchford stations. Today part of the trackbed of the branch and the first section of the trackbed into the mine are still walkable, being in Irthlingborough's Country Park.

Above **Irthlingborough station looking towards Peterborough in April 1954.** *H. C. Casserley*

Below **Old stone sleepers used in the early days of the L&B recycled as stepping stones from Ringstead & Addington station towards Addington village, photographed in the 1980s.** *Author*

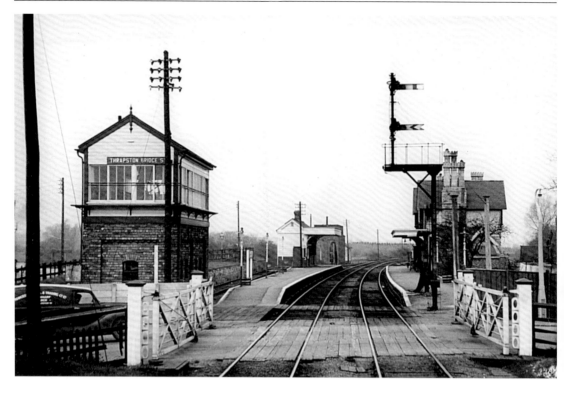

Above Thrapston Bridge Street station looking towards Peterborough in April 1954. *H. C. Casserley*

Below Barnwell station in May 1973. The waiting room starred in a TV commercial prior to being moved to Wansford on the NVR. *Author*

Above **Elton station looking towards Peterborough in April 1959.** *H. C. Casserley*

Below **An early photograph of Ditchford station.** *Author's collection*

No history of this part of the county would be complete without mention of the famous Ditchford Treacle Mines! These are now well-established in local folklore, yet quite how this came about is somewhat obscure. In 1875 and 1877 the LNWR installed sidings at Ditchford for a Mr Whitehouse. Ironstone quarrying took place in the vicinity and the sidings were obviously provided to serve the quarry. It has been suggested that the ore was of a treacly consistency, but no one is sure. Because of the remoteness of Ditchford station, the Station Master was authorised to stop trains in order that his family could reach Wellingborough, and for most of its life fresh water was delivered each day by train.

Passenger services consisted principally of five trains each way Monday to Saturday, with two on Sunday. There were other shuttle services between Blisworth and Northampton,

Wellingborough's first station – London Road – in April 1960. The silos of Whitworth's Flour Mill can be seen on the left. *R. M. Casserley*

a pattern that was to remain in force for most of the line's history.

In 1857 the MR built its new line from Wigston to Hitchin, and in so doing crossed the Peterborough line at Wellingborough; here the MR built a connecting spur from the south of its station to the east end of the LNWR station and began using this for goods services. In 1861 the LNWR informed the MR that it intended to use the powers that it had already been granted to start running its trains from Wichnor, south of Burton, to Burton-on-Trent itself, where it had a short isolated section of railway. The MR responded by announcing that it would take up its powers to introduce a passenger service between Wellingborough and Northampton. This arrangement was acceptable to both parties, so the MR bought some land in Northampton and erected a small station near the LNWR's Bridge Street facility (the 'Bridge Street' suffix was added in 1876) with a connection to the LNWR line near Hardingstone. This small structure had a

Northampton Bridge Street station in July 1959.
R. M. Casserley

very short life: opened in October 1866, it closed in June 1872 with the arrival of the MR line from Bedford and the opening of the new station at St John's Street.

With the arrival of the MR at Northampton from Wellingborough, passengers now had the choice of a faster service by the MR. In 1903 the average journey time was 17 minutes, while the LNWR took 27 minutes. For Wellingborough passengers it meant that whichever station they used, they still had quite a long walk into the town centre. In early MR days some trains did work between Northampton and Kettering, but essentially it was a Wellingborough-Northampton service.

The Grouping in 1923 appears to have made little difference to the pattern of services between the two towns, but it was not until the early 1960s that one or two trains started working again between Northampton, Kettering and on to Leicester. By then it was too late to attempt to think

about how services could be improved, because BR announced in July 1963 that it was proposing to withdraw the passenger services between Northampton, Peterborough and Wellingborough as from 9 September of that year.

There followed the usual objections from various groups, including many children who travelled to Wellingborough Grammar and High Schools from stations mainly to the east of Wellingborough. However, despite much opposition the result was what had been expected from the outset: closure would take place except for the section between Peterborough and Oundle, the latter acting as a small railhead for freight, mainly coal. There is no doubt that one of the principal points of the case for closure was the number of level crossings en route and the costs involved in manning them. The authorities promised a substitute bus service, but that was really a non-starter from the beginning.

So on Saturday 2 May 1964, some seven months later than originally planned, the last passenger trains ran. Well, not quite. Someone obviously with some political clout was able

Wansford station in pre-preservation days, April 1959.
H. C. Casserley

to bring pressure on BR to allow end-of-term special trains to run from Oundle to Peterborough for the benefit of pupils of Oundle School! In fact, these trains ran until 1972. In November of that year BR closed Oundle as a goods depot; although there had been some freight movements over the line, these had ceased by 1969 (apart from the eastern end, as already mentioned). For some time around 1968/9 the tracks between Wellingborough and Irthlingborough were used to store hundreds of disused wagons.

Today it is still possible to trace and walk parts of the trackbed. Castle Ashby goods shed has been transformed into a restaurant (complete with a static coach to add to the railway atmosphere), but it is at the eastern end, between Yarwell Junction and Peterborough, that is of interest today. Around the time of closure, a group of railway enthusiasts started a process that was to become the Nene Valley Railway, with its headquarters at Wansford.

Elsewhere it is still possible to walk various lengths of the trackbed. The nature reserve at Summer Leys (between Wollaston and Great Doddington) and the new Stanwick Lakes both use part of the trackbed as part of their new trails.

RUGBY TO STAMFORD

Although most of this branch lay just outside the northern boundaries of the county, two of its 11 stations, at Stanford Hall (later Yelvertoft & Stanford Hall) and Medbourne Bridge (Ashley & Weston after 1878), were just in the county.

Like the Peterborough branch, which used the Nene Valley, this line used the Welland for its route. Had it come up the southern side of the valley, Rockingham, very much a county village, would have had

Rockingham station was just across the River Welland in Rutland. Note the characteristic LNWR signal and signal box, photographed in July 1965. *Les Hanson*

its station in the county. As it was, the villagers had to walk a mile across the valley floor to reach their station, which was almost in Caldecott.

The branch was intended to reach Stamford, but would need to use the Syston to Peterborough branch of the Midland Railway (MR), which had opened in 1846, from Luffenham to reach its destination. The line was the last to be promoted by the London & Birmingham Railway before it became part of the London & North Western Railway (LNWR), obtaining its Act in June 1846, a month before the amalgamation.

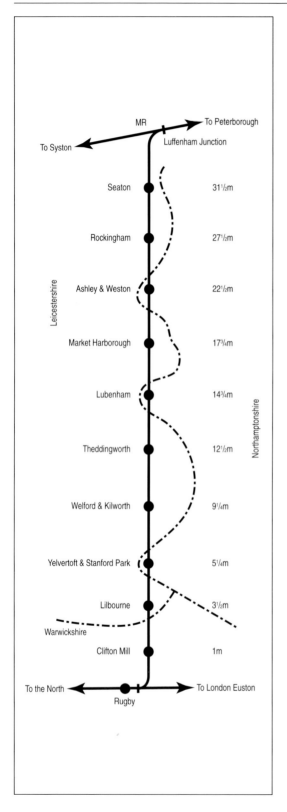

Rugby to Stamford (LNWR), opened throughout in June 1851 (distances from Rugby).

Consequently all the construction work was done by the new company.

Like the Peterborough branch, it was conceived as a single line but with provision being made to double the line, if needed, at a later date. While using the Welland Valley to keep construction costs down, the penalty was the number of crossing places encountered en route.

The line was built in stages. The first section to be opened was that between Rugby and Market Harborough, which opened in May 1850. Market Harborough to Rockingham opened a month later, while the final section, on to Luffenham, had to wait for a further year. Doubling of the line was not completed until July 1878.

Of the 11 stations on the line, only two remain open today, at Rugby and Market Harborough. It was at these two stations where the most significant changes were to take place during the life of the branch. At Rugby, trains coming off the branch had to cross over all the main lines to the south of the station in order to reach the down (western) platforms. These operating problems increased when the loop line from Rugby to Northampton opened in December 1881. To overcome this the LNWR applied to Parliament for an Act that would enable it to build a flyover at the south end of Rugby station and to build a single-track viaduct of some 13 arches, which would curve into the main lines from a junction at Clifton Mill, the first station on the branch. This work demonstrates just how important the potential of the branch was seen to be by the LNWR. The new works came into use in July 1885, and both are still extant, the flyover still in daily use and the viaduct now sitting astride a golf course.

At Market Harborough nothing of any significance was to take place for seven years

Rugby to Stamford (LNWR), opened throughout in June 1851 (distances from Rugby).

Right Lilbourne station in April 1965, looking towards Market Harborough with the new M1 motorway in the background. This was another station just outside the county boundary.
H. C. Casserley

Right Welford & Kilworth station, facing Market Harborough in April 1965. *R. M. Casserley*

Below Lubenham station looking towards Market Harborough, also in April 1965. *R. M. Casserley*

Seaton station in August 1965. The notice reads 'To open the gates ring the bell for porter', which suggests that the gates were normally closed to road traffic. *Les Hanson*

between the branch opening and the arrival of the MR in 1857. Here the roles were reversed. As already stated, the LNWR would have to use the MR to gain access to Stamford, and now the MR was to use a section of the LNWR line from a point north of Market Harborough station to another junction immediately south of the station, both companies using the same station.

However, with the growth of traffic, especially on the MR, this section of line became a bottleneck and something had to be done. The MR decided to build a flyover where its line joined the LNWR north of the station, and to construct its own lines to the southern junction; this would remove all the conflicting movements of traffic.

Prior to these new lines opening the two companies decided that they would need a new station; this would be jointly owned and each company would have its own platforms and staff. The new station, described as being

Rugby, Market Harborough, and Stamford.—L. & N. W.

WEEK DAYS ONLY.	a m	p m	p m	p m	WEEK DAYS ONLY.	a m	a m	p m	p m
Birmingham	7 35	12 25	4 0	6 0	Stamford	6 20	8 50	2 0	5 0
London	6 15	11 0	2 45	5 10	Luffenham	6 32	9 2	2 12	5 12
NORTHAMPTON	7 25	12 20	3 20	5 38	Uppingham (by coach)	—	8 35	1 35	4 35
Rugby	8 45	1 50	5 0	7 50	Seaton and Uppingham	6 41	9 12	2 22	5 21
Lilbourne (arrive)	8 53	1 58	5 8	7 58	Rockingham	6 50	9 22	2 30	5 30
Yelvertoft	8 59	2 4	5 14	8 4	Medbourn Bridge	7 1	9 33	2 41	5 41
Welford (for Lut'wrth)	9 6	2 11	5 21	8 11	Market Harboro' { arr.	7 12	9 45	2 51	5 52
Theddingworth	9 16	2 21	5 31	8 21	Market Harboro' { dep.	7 15	9 51	3 0	6 0
Lubenham	9 22	2 28	5 37	8 27	Lubenham	7 20	9 56	3 5	6 5
Market Harboro' { arr.	9 30	2 36	5 45	8 35	Theddingworth	7 25	10 3	3 12	6 12
Market Harboro' { dep.	9 44	2 40	5 47	8 48	Welford (for Lut'wrth)	7 33	10 12	3 21	6 21
Medbourne Bridge	9 56	2 51	5 59	9 0	Yelvertoft	7 41	10 21	3 30	6 30
Rockingham	10 8	3 3	6 11	9 12	Lilbourne	7 46	10 26	3 35	6 35
Seaton and Uppingham	10 18	3 12	6 21	9 22	Rugby	7 55	10 35	3 45	6 45
Uppingham (by coach)	11 0	4 0	6 55	—	NORTHAMPTON	9 25	11 45	5 50	8 25
Luffenham	10 26	3 20	6 29	9 30	London	10 30	12 50	7 15	9 15
Stamford	10 41	3 35	6 45	9 45	Birmingham	9 20	12 5	6 10	8 10

Trains stop at Clifton Mill by signal only.

An 1873 timetable for the branch.
Author's collection

in the 'domestic Georgian style', opened in September 1884, though it was not completed until February 1886. In between those two dates, in June 1885, the MR opened its new flyover and associated trackworks. Perhaps the surprising thing was that in the early days it was possible for MR traffic to use the LNWR lines to Rugby, but with the advent of the new MR lines no direct connections were put in place; all through traffic had to go via the exchange sidings, which became quite extensive. It was not until 1924 that a double junction was installed, and of course by then both companies had become part of the London Midland & Scottish Railway (LMS) in 1923, which removed the old rivalries.

Passenger traffic over the branch was never great, consisting of only a few trains each way on weekdays and a couple on Sundays. As with all lines, the amount of goods traffic is more difficult to quantify. From the earliest days public timetables for the passenger services were available, but not so the goods, but we can be sure that this traffic rose much faster than the passenger side of the business.

One great advantage for the new branch was that LNWR traffic from the north destined for Peterborough and the Eastern

Theddingworth station, with the original crossing gates in situ in August 2002. The signal box has been converted into living accommodation. *Author*

Counties no longer had to be worked to Blisworth, then reversed on to the Peterborough branch. Having said that, it must be remembered that the LNWR still had to use the MR lines between Luffenham, Stamford and Peterborough. Like all its competitors, the LNWR was always looking to see how it could expand its empire or operate its system more efficiently; in the latter case we shall see how the LNWR tackled this problem when we look at the Seaton–Yarwell line.

In June 1904 the LNWR opened extensive sidings at Welham, purely for handling the increasing coal traffic that was coming off the GNR/LNWR joint line from the Nottinghamshire and Derbyshire coalfields.

The branch was one of many that closed in the 1950s and '60s. Ashley & Weston station was the first to close in June 1951, followed by Clifton Mill in April 1953. Most of the goods facilities closed in 1964, while the remaining passenger services survived until June 1966.

Several of the stations on the branch are now in private hands, with one enterprising owner using the space between the platforms as a swimming pool! (This might be a good opportunity to remind readers that the surviving stations are privately owned and permission should be sought to visit or to do any photography.)

NORTHAMPTON TO MARKET HARBOROUGH

As we have already noted, Northampton's first station opened in May 1845 on the line from Blisworth to Peterborough. That same year a somewhat more grandiose scheme was afoot in the shape of the South Midland Railway, which would have been a joint venture between the fledgling Midland Railway (MR) and the London & Birmingham L&B, from 1846 part of the London & North Western Railway (LNWR). This new line would have run from south of Northampton to north of Leicester. However, the redoubtable George Hudson was in control of the MR at that time and he subsequently had other ideas and the plan came to nothing. One of his plans did, however, come to fruition, namely the 1857 line from Leicester to Hitchin via Market Harborough, Kettering, Wellingborough and Bedford. Once again Northampton had lost its chance of being on a main line.

However, at the beginning of the 1850s large quantities of good-quality iron ore were being discovered all over the county and the railways were to play a key role in the transportation of the ore to the foundries. In August 1853 the LNWR obtained an Act to build a branch from a point some 1,200 yards west of its existing station at Northampton to a junction with its Rugby & Stamford branch, some 700 yards west of its Market Harborough station, the length being just over 18 miles. Amazingly, no provision was made initially for a station in Northampton on this new branch, being seen by the

LNWR as a Blisworth to Market Harborough service.

In August 1858 it was reported that the LNWR would use its station on the Peterborough line (known as Northampton Bridge Street from 1876), but this would involve running into the station, then reversing to the junction and reversing again in order to proceed towards Market Harborough, and vice versa!

Colonel Yolland, the Inspecting Officer for the Board of Trade, was not happy with this arrangement. It is clear that the LNWR did not consider Northampton to be very important, but Col Yolland's report made the company have second thoughts, because by October of that same year he reported that, 'The roadside station at Northampton has been commenced, but is still incomplete and there are no station buildings.' This station was to become known as Northampton Castle.

There were also other problems, including wooden viaducts that were not strong enough to carry some of the heavier locomotives and no turntables at either Blisworth or Market Harborough. Without these, locomotives would have to run tender-first in one direction.

When the branch opened in February 1859 Northampton had its second station, but with no goods facilities. This, said the LNWR, could still be dealt with at its other station.

On the branch there were stations at Pitsford & Brampton, Brixworth, Lamport and Kelmarsh. Like so many new lines being built at this time, the route was laid out for double track, but was single when opened. Under normal circumstances laying an additional track is not too difficult, but this branch had two tunnels en route, at Oxendon and Kelmarsh, 462 and 322 yards long respectively. The problem was that the LNWR built them as single-bore tunnels, which meant that when the line was doubled new tunnels had to be built. This short-sightedness can still be seen today!

Like the Peterborough branch, the new line to Market Harborough used the valley floor. This meant that the route was almost flat, but that the villages it served were on the higher ground on either side of the line, and the line would again, like that to Peterborough, suffer from the many roads that crossed the valley linking the various communities. Initially this did not present too many operating problems since there were only two passenger trains a day in both directions. However, when the line was under construction iron ore was discovered in at least three locations adjacent to the line, and this quickly resulted in extra traffic.

Within a few years of the opening, the villagers of Clipston and the immediate area were pressing the LNWR for their own station. Although it was only a few miles to either Market Harborough or Kelmarsh stations, it should be borne in mind that in those days the majority of people had only their feet to get them around the countryside! The LNWR agreed to their request and Clipston(e) & Oxendon station opened in June 1863.

This success was not lost on the inhabitants of Spratton. In the original plans they were going to have a station on the Spratton–Brixworth road, but the LNWR decided to build a station on the Brixworth–Cottesbrooke road. So the Sprattonians petitioned the LNWR for a station on the original site, and surprisingly, bearing in mind

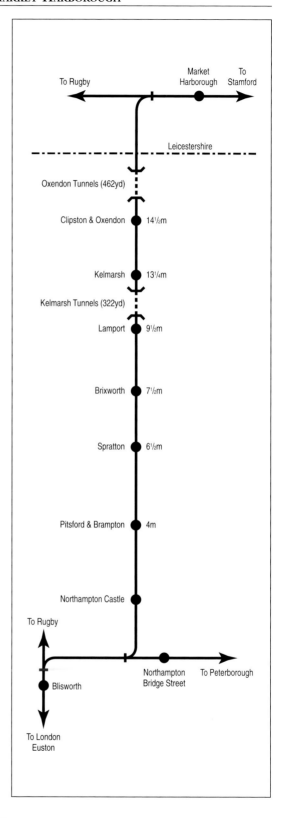

Northampton to Market Harborough (LNWR), opened in February 1859 (distances from Northampton Castle).

Left **Brixworth station, looking towards Northampton in June 1955.** *H. C. Casserley*

Below **The very similar Lamport station was photographed from the same train.** *H. C. Casserley*

that Brixworth station was less than a mile away by rail, the company agreed; however, it said that the station would be basic, nothing more than a wooden platform, and it was to be for six months only. In the event the amount of traffic generated must have been far greater than the LNWR ever envisaged, because after the trial period it agreed to the erection of a permanent station. Spratton station opened in March 1864, and because of its close proximity to Brixworth it never had any goods facilities.

The years 1845-52 are often referred to as the years of 'The Railway Mania'. In that period many lines were projected and built, with, in some cases, several different companies building their own lines to a single destination, such was the desire to get their share of the traffic. Sometimes common sense prevailed and two companies would agree to

Right The southern end of the up-line tunnel at Oxendon in May 1974. *Author*

Right The situation today! *Author*

Below One of several level crossings along the route, Boughton Crossing in July 1974 was little changed from previous decades. *Author*

Clipston & Oxendon station in April 1965 with a solitary passenger waiting for a Northampton train. *R. M. Casserley*

a formal joint arrangement whereby they agreed to allow each other's traffic to use each other's lines and stations. One such agreement between the LNWR and the Great Northern Railway (GNR) was to affect the Northampton-Market Harborough branch.

In 1874 the GNR/LNWR Joint line received its Act to build a line from Newark to Welham, a few miles from Market Harborough on the LNWR's Rugby-Stamford line. When this line opened in 1879 the LNWR had easier access to the lucrative coal traffic from the Nottingham and Derbyshire coalfields and could run its trains to Nottingham, while the GNR would have access to Northampton. The LNWR had decided as early as April 1860 to double the line between Northampton and Market Harborough, but only as far as Lamport; as we have seen, the section from there to Market Harborough would have meant boring two more tunnels. However, with this new traffic flow pending, the decision was made to construct the two tunnels and finish the doubling of the line. The tunnels were completed and opened for traffic in August 1879.

We now switch our attention to the southern end of the line. In the 1870s the LNWR was facing congestion on its main line from Rugby to London and had decided to quadruple the route. The normal practice was to lay the new set of lines next to the existing ones, but in this case the decision was taken to route the new pair of lines through Northampton. This would at last stop the clamouring from the inhabitants for their town to be on a main line, albeit only on a loop. This solution avoided having to tunnel at Kilsby again! This new line would merge with the Market Harborough branch a few miles north of Northampton at Kingsthorpe (see the chapter on the Northampton Loop).

As already stated, when the branch opened there were only two services a day. The number slowly increased with the passage of time, with, perhaps, the 1920s seeing the greatest number. A timetable for 1921 shows five Northampton-Nottingham trains on weekdays, with a through coach to and from Melton Mowbray on one service each way to Euston. Obviously this was an attempt to compete with the MR's services via Kettering to St Pancras.

Over the years the number of iron-ore quarries opening in the vicinity of the line –

An early BR timetable issued in April 1949, showing through trains to Melton Mowbray and Nottingham.
Author

in the Spratton, Pitsford, Brixworth and Lamport areas – created new traffic flows. Also, in what is believed to have been a Second World War measure, the Air Ministry opened a petrol storage depot at Kelmarsh with a siding for the depot.

In 1923, when the Grouping took place, the MR and the LNWR became part of the new London Midland & Scottish Railway (LMS). One of the early decisions of this new company was to reinstate the junctions at Market Harborough so that through running was possible between the two lines, as had been possible in the very early days. This meant that southbound trains on the MR could be diverted to Euston and northbound trains from Euston could be diverted to the old Midland lines. It also enabled new services to be run, especially during the holiday seasons.

Sadly, the increase in road traffic was beginning to be felt on rail services and the more rural lines felt it keenly. The first closure on the branch came on 23 May 1949 at Spratton. Then, in December 1953, the joint line from Welham northwards closed, and with it went the services to Nottingham (Victoria). To offset this loss, some trains were run to Nottingham via the Midland lines from Market Harborough.

January 1960 saw the closure of the remaining intermediate stations on the branch, together with most of the goods services. The track was left in situ, however, and continued to see use for goods services and as a diversionary route. Then, at the beginning of 1969, the line was used for a diverted St Pancras-Glasgow sleeper service and its return working. Enthusiasts were known to catch the down service just to ride over the line once more! Finally, an enthusiasts' special traversed the branch for

PASSENGER TRAIN SERVICES

FROM

NORTHAMPTON

TO

MARKET HARBOROUGH, MELTON MOWBRAY & NOTTINGHAM

FROM 2nd MAY 1949 UNTIL FURTHER NOTICE

FROM	TIMES OF DEPARTURE			
	am	am	pm	pm
NORTHAMPTON (Castle).. .. .. dep	6 40	9 10	1 20	..
PITSFORD & BRAMPTON	6 47	9 17	1 29	..
SPRATTON	6 52	9 22	1 34	..
BRIXWORTH	6 54	9 24	1 36	..
LAMPORT	6 59	9 29	1 41	..
KELMARSH..	7 6	9 36	1 48	..
CLIPSTON & OXENDON	7 10	9 39	1 51	..
MARKET HARBOROUGH .. .. { arr	7 18	9 46	1 58	..
{ dep	7 56	9 53	..	2 45
MELTON MOWBRAY ... ... { arr	8 51	10 48	..	3 37
{ dep	8 53	10 50	..	3 41
NOTTINGHAM (L.R.) (L.L.) ... ... arr	9 44	12 01	..	4 32

RETURN ARRANGEMENTS
SEE NOTICES POSTED AT DEPARTING STATIONS

For LUGGAGE ALLOWANCES see Regulations and Conditions.

BRITISH RAILWAYS

April, 1949
B.R. 35000

the last time in August 1981. By then a preservation society had been formed to try and save the line, but this is dealt with in a further section.

In 1882, when the Blisworth-Peterborough trains were diverted into the new Castle station at Northampton, the LNWR introduced a shuttle service between Blisworth and Northampton, which meant that passengers could transfer easily between the services. This service closed at the same time as the Northampton-Market Harborough stopping services.

Today most of the route between Northampton (Boughton Crossing) and Market Harborough is a public footpath called 'The Brampton Valley Way', a distance of some 14 miles, the sole remaining section of the original branch being that between Northampton and Kingsthorpe.

SEATON TO YARWELL JUNCTION

As already stated, the London & North Western Railway (LNWR) was, like all the major companies, always looking for ways to improve its services at the expense of its rivals if at all possible. Accordingly, it considered ways of reaching Peterborough without using the Midland Railway between Luffenham and Peterborough. The answer was to build its own line from Seaton to a point west of Wansford on its original branch from Blisworth (this represented the shortest distance between the two lines, Seaton and Wansford being only 13 miles apart). However, it meant crossing the higher ground between the Welland and Nene valleys, which some drivers referred to as 'going over the Alps'.

The LNWR obtained its Act of Parliament in July 1873 and three intermediate stations – at Wakerley & Barrowden, Kings Cliffe and Nassington – were opened to traffic on 1 November 1879.

Now the LNWR had two routes to Peterborough, with the added bonus of a reduction in the mileage, and once the new line was up and running the Seaton-Luffenham line lost its importance; it was singled in July 1907, although the station at Morcott managed to stay open until June 1966.

As time passed the new line took on a new importance, seeing through services to Harwich from the Midlands and specials to the seaside, etc, then, during the Second World War, as a diversionary route. The Great Northern Railway (GNR) had running powers over the line, and from July 1883 to April 1916 it ran a service from Leicester (Belgrave Road) to Peterborough using the north-to-east part of the triangular junction at Welham (opened in July 1883); whether the GNR trains stopped at the LNWR stations is not known.

Kings Cliffe in May 1937: admittedly not much of a view of the station, but it is a nice shot of Johnson 0-4-4T No 1422 with a train for Peterborough.
H. C. Casserley

Right **Seaton to Yarwell Junction (LNWR), opened in November 1879 (distances from Seaton).**

Closure to passenger services came in July 1957 for Nassington and June 1966 for the other two stations. Nassington was to become well known because of the iron-ore quarries in the area. Surprisingly these did not open until the summer of 1939 and continued until the end of 1970. By then the railway preservation movement was in full swing and the quarries' final days were marked by a series of special trains over the remaining system and the purchase of several of the locomotives by preservation groups.

British Railways had lifted much of the track by 1968, but one section was left in situ and used by the Nassington Barrowden Mining Co Ltd to access a new quarry that opened in 1969.

Wakerley & Barrowden station has been saved and is in private hands, otherwise there is little left to show of what was once an important link in our railway system.

Below **Wakerley & Barrowden station in November 1999 after the removal of the trackbed and most of the embankment.** *Author*

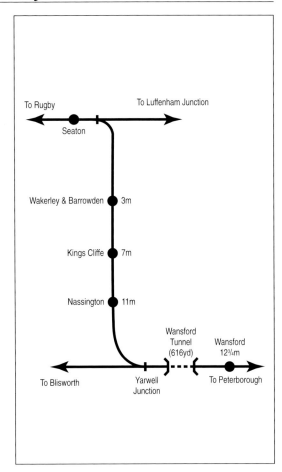

WEEDON TO LEAMINGTON SPA

As early as 1845 the London & Birmingham Railway had surveyed a new line from Weedon to Daventry, but then it seems to have forgotten about it; one suspects that its main focus was its branches eastwards from its main line. In August 1846, after its incorporation as part of the London & North Western Railway (LNWR) in July of that year, it obtained an

Act of Parliament, which, it was expected, would include the new line to Daventry; however, the Act only covered a proposal for a new line from Weedon to Hardingstone (Northampton) on the Peterborough branch. This would mean that north-to-east traffic would not have to reverse at Blisworth in order to reach the branch, but this Act was allowed to lapse; it was to be the Rugby to Peterborough route via Market Harborough and Stamford, and ultimately the cut-off route from Seaton to Wansford, that would provide this facility.

Thirty-nine years were to elapse before the

Weedon's second station in September 1956: 'Jubilee' Class No 45647 *Sturdee* calls at the down main-line platform with a Bletchley-Rugby local while Ivatt No 41228 waits in the bay with the connection to Leamington. *R. M. Casserley*

Right **Weedon to Leamington Spa (LNWR), opened throughout in August 1895 (distances from Weedon).**

LNWR once more turned its attention to Daventry, although in 1862 an independent company, the Daventry Railway, had obtained its Act, but this also lapsed with nothing being done. So, in July 1885, the LNWR obtained an Act that also allowed the company to build a new station at Weedon, necessary because the original station site was somewhat cramped and it would have been difficult to find the space for a bay platform for the branch. However, all that happened was that the new station was built just to the north of the A45 road, instead of slightly south. Today remains of the first station can still be seen, together with the reasons why it had to be moved.

The Act also allowed for the removal of the old bridge that had been built on the L&B's line over the canal leading to Weedon Barracks. Recent research has revealed that this bridge was designed to be slid horizontally out of the way to allow canal traffic to pass – what would current health and safety regulations have made of this arrangement? The track was subsequently raised to allow the construction of a fixed bridge over the canal.

It appears to have been normal practice for

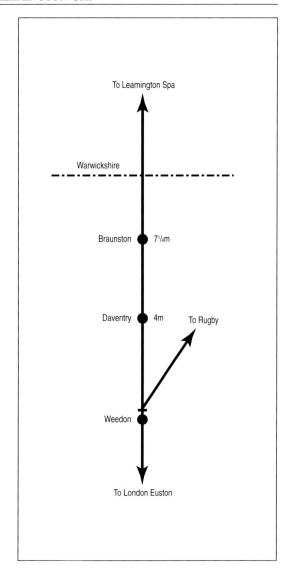

Below **A 1921 timetable for the branch.** *Author's collection*

WEEDON, DAVENTRY, AND LEAMINGTON SPA BRANCH.

Week Days only.

	a.m.		a.m	p.m.	p.m.		p.m.	p.m.	p.m.	
London (Euston) depart	6 45	.	9 30	.	12 15	.	2 5	4 15	5 40	.
Northampton (Castle) ,,	8 30	.	11 56	12 55	4 10	.	4 10	6 0	7 5	.
Blisworth ,,	8 45	.	12 11	1 10	4 30	.	4 40	6 18	7 31	.
Weedon ....depart	9 10	.	12 23	1 22	4 40	.	5 15	6 30	8 0	.
Daventry { arrive	9 18	.	12 28	1 32	4 50	.	5 23	6 40	8 8	.
Daventry { depart	9 20	.	12 34	.	.	.	5 24	.	8 14	.
Braunston	9 28	.	12 42	.	.	.	5 32	.	8 23	.
Flecknoe	9 34	.	12 48	.	.	.	5 38	.	8 30	.
Napton & Stockton	9 44	.	12 56	.	.	.	5 46	.	8 38	.
Southam & Long Itchington	9 53	.	1 3	.	.	.	5 52	.	8 50	.
Leamington Spa ... arrive	10 11	.	1 25	.	.	.	6 15	.	9 12	.
Warwick (Milverton) ,,	10 22	.	1 30	.	.	.	6 a36	.	9 18	.

Week Days only.

		a.m.		a.m.	p.m	p.m	p.m	p.m	p.m
Warwick (Milverton) depart	. . .	6 58	.	9 20	. . .	3 0	. . .	6 0
Leamington Spa ...... ,,	.	7 7	.	9 25	.	3 5	.	6 27
Southam & Long Itchington	. . .	7 23	.	9 41	. .	3 21	.	6 43
Napton & Stockton	. . .	7 29	.	9 47	. .	3 28	.	6 49
Flecknoe	. . .	7 36	.	9 55	. .	3 36	.	6 56
Braunston	. . .	7 43	.	10 2	. .	3 43	.	7 3
Daventry ...... { arrive	. . .	7 51	.	10 10	. .	3 52	.	7 14
Daventry ...... { depart	.	7 54	.	10 20	1 56	3 53	5 0	7 5	7 19
Weedon ....arrive	.	8 3	.	10 30	. .	2 44	2 5	3 7	18	7 28
Blisworth ....arrive	.	8 17	.	10 43	2 20	4 11	5 53	7 33	7 52
Northampton (Castle) ,,	. . .	8 33	.	11 5	. .	2 36	5 5	6 15	7 50	8 10
London (Euston)... ,,	.	10 15	.	12 25	.	5 35	6 30	7 55	.	10 15

a.—On Saturdays arrives Warwick 6.49 p.m.

the LNWR to plan its branches for double track but to start with a single track. The branch was just over 3 miles long and opened for both passenger and goods traffic on 1 March 1888. By now railways were almost commonplace, but this did not stop the local population enjoying the usual junketings!

For almost all of the way from Weedon to Daventry the line was on a rising gradient of 1 in 80, which, when coupled with some sharp curves, ensured that it would remain only as a minor branch line all its life.

In 1890 the LNWR obtained a further Act to extend the line from Daventry to Leamington, joining the company's Rugby-Leamington branch 'at or near Ridgeway Lane' (Marton Junction). With a length of just over 14 miles, the extension opened in August 1895. Even with this link open, the line never saw any great amount of traffic; in fact, it was said that at one time there was as much goods traffic, including cattle for the market at Daventry, as there was passenger business!

For a few months between 1901 and 1902 a coach off the 5.35pm Euston-Liverpool express was slipped at Weedon and was worked through to Leamington on a later train. Considering that Leamington had been reached from London via the Great Western Railway in 1852, one can understand why this service had such a short life.

A further attempt to improve the service came in 1906 when a steam railcar, capable of carrying 50 passengers, started operating, but it only lasted for two months. The railcars were poor steamers, and the gradients were too much for them. In 1910 a two-coach pull-and-push service started operating, and this was to be the norm for the rest of the branch's life. The passenger services never reached more than six or seven trains a day, with no Sunday services; of these, nearly half only went as far as Daventry. The final years of the branch saw some services working through to Blisworth, with one or two reversing at Blisworth and continuing to Northampton. Closure of the branch came in September 1958.

Until 2004 it was possible to see a superb O gauge model of Daventry station in that town's museum. Sadly the museum closed in that year and the whereabouts of the model are not known.

The model of Daventry station that used to be housed in the town's museum. *Author*

NORTHAMPTON LOOP

When the London & Birmingham line opened in 1838, it is doubtful if anyone could have predicted how the section of line between Rugby and London was to become one of the main railway arteries of the country, even into the 21st century. Within a decade of its opening other lines arrived at Rugby from the north, principally the Trent Valley route of the London & North Western Railway (LNWR) from Stafford. Additionally, until 1857 the Midland Railway had used its Leicester to Rugby line to get its traffic to London over the LNWR. This increasing congestion meant that the LNWR had no alternative but to seek Parliamentary approval to quadruple the route from Rugby to London, but one of the first things to be considered was which way to go.

In 1875 the LNWR obtained the Act that gave it permission to build a new line from Rugby to Roade via Northampton; it might have been possible to use the existing line from Northampton to Blisworth, but this would have meant very tight curves, both at Northampton and Blisworth. Instead the new line would go straight on from Northampton, cross the Peterborough branch, tunnel beneath Hunsbury Hill and meet the original route at the north end of Roade cutting. Not only was this cutting to be enlarged, but in order to keep the gradients on the new lines to a minimum the new cutting would be deeper than the original pair of lines. When one considers that this was all done by hand, one can only marvel.

Between Rugby and Northampton two tunnels were needed, at Crick and Watford Lodge, 595 and 115 yards long respectively. Three stations were built, at Kilsby & Crick, Long Buckby and Althorp Park. The route used the tracks of the Market Harborough branch from Kingsthorpe into Northampton. Northampton's Castle station was by now totally inadequate; although a few enhancements had been made, a new station would have to be built.

Northampton had had a castle since the end of the 11th century and, although not much of it remained by the time the railway arrived on the scene, there were no organisations like the National Trust to protect what had survived! Before the building of the new station could begin it was necessary to divert the River Nene, which had previously flowed by the walls of the castle. The LNWR therefore bought the castle area and used the historic site to accommodate its new goods depot. As a sop to the townsfolk, the company moved the Postern Gate – one of the few remaining parts left standing – to a new site, and thankfully it can still be seen today near the main entrance to the station.

The new line opened in August 1881, but for goods traffic only. In that same year the LNWR was granted permission to quadruple the line from its junction with the Market Harborough line to Northampton station. Passenger services started at the beginning of December 1881, but only between Rugby

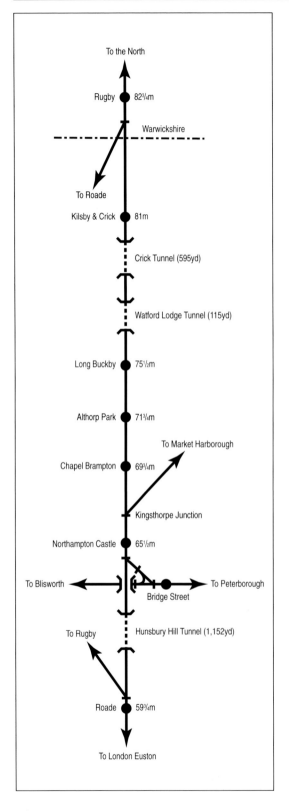

and Northampton; one wonders if the new cutting at Roade was not considered safe enough for passenger trains. Eventually, in April 1882, full services started. Northampton, at last, had a direct link to London. In November 1891 the LNWR's fears concerning the safety of the new section of Roade cutting were justified, when, after a period of heavy rain, a landslip filled the new cutting. It was to be five months later, in April 1892, before the hundreds of navvies managed to clear the line, and, to ensure that it did not happen again, overhead iron girders were used to brace the cutting sides. It is worth visiting the area today to see just what was done and what was achieved by hand.

Also worth a visit is the Pulpit Bridge, just north of Watford village. It was built at the time of the opening of the Loop line, and not only boasts four cast-iron pulpits on each corner, but also carries the coat of arms of the Henley family, through whose land the railway passed. It is said that the pulpits were used by the local clergy to address the local parishioners.

Included in the 1875 Act for the new line was permission to build a short spur from the south of Northampton station to a point west of Bridge Street station. This had opened by April 1880 for goods traffic and in April 1882 for passenger services, at the same time as the opening of the new Northampton Castle station. As mentioned in the Market Harborough and Peterborough chapters, this meant that Peterborough trains could run into Castle station, making easier connections for passengers.

In May 1912 a new station was opened on the Loop at Church Brampton, between Northampton and Althorp Park. Quite what the rationale was for opening this station is unsure, but suffice to say that it did not stay open for long, closing on 1 January 1917. The

Northampton Loop (LNWR), opened throughout in April 1882 (distances from London Euston).

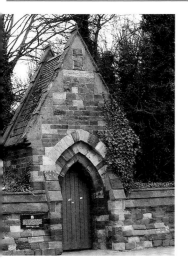

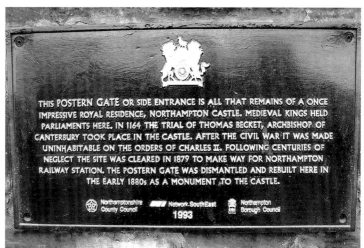

THIS POSTERN GATE OR SIDE ENTRANCE IS ALL THAT REMAINS OF A ONCE IMPRESSIVE ROYAL RESIDENCE, NORTHAMPTON CASTLE. MEDIEVAL KINGS HELD PARLIAMENTS HERE. IN 1164 THE TRIAL OF THOMAS BECKET, ARCHBISHOP OF CANTERBURY TOOK PLACE IN THE CASTLE. AFTER THE CIVIL WAR IT WAS MADE UNINHABITABLE ON THE ORDERS OF CHARLES II. FOLLOWING CENTURIES OF NEGLECT THE SITE WAS CLEARED IN 1879 TO MAKE WAY FOR NORTHAMPTON RAILWAY STATION. THE POSTERN GATE WAS DISMANTLED AND REBUILT HERE IN THE EARLY 1880s AS A MONUMENT TO THE CASTLE.

Northamptonshire County Council   Network SouthEast   Northampton Borough Council
1993

Above **The sole remaining part of the castle at Northampton, the Postern Gate, is now situated just outside the present station, together with an explanatory plaque.** *Both Author*

Right **The roadside booking hall at Long Buckby in April 1965.** *R. M. Casserley*

Below **Long Buckby station, with its awnings cut back with the electrification of the route in April 1965.** *R. M. Casserley*

Althorp Park in July 1959, just another typical LNWR station at first glance from platform level, but seen from the outside it takes on a more important appearance due to the nearby Spencer family home at Althorp. *Both H. C. Casserley*

The unique pulpit bridge at Watford, with two of the cast iron pulpits very evident in this October 1993 view. *Author*

station was close to Northampton Golf Club and it is claimed that pressure from the golfers brought about its re-opening in May 1919! However, with the end of the First World War came the steady growth of the motor car, and the golfers preferred their new toys to travelling by train. Consequently the station closed for a second time in May 1931.

As already mentioned, the Grouping of 1923 had little effect on Northampton since, of the five services that ran into Castle station, three were previously LNWR and the other two Midland Railway (MR), and these were now all part of the new LMS.

Northampton station, like its MR counterpart at Wellingborough, was 65 miles from London, and the MR had made Wellingborough its halfway point for coal traffic from the Derby, Nottingham and Yorkshire coalfields to London. Northampton

was to see a similar situation in the early 1930s when the LMS decided that it was a good location for new freight concentration/sorting sidings. To this end a new marshalling yard was built on the down side, north of Castle station. The new lines were designated as slow lines and were partly built, dare one say it, to keep freight traffic off the main line. The result was that passenger services never enjoyed the same importance as those on the main line, and remain so today, although for different reasons.

The LNWR built two locomotive depots in Northampton. The first, built in 1853 on the Peterborough branch west of Bridge Street station, still stands today. The second and larger one was built in the triangle of land bounded by the Blisworth, Peterborough and Castle station lines. Opened in 1881, at the time of the opening of the Loop line through the town, it disappeared with the passing of steam in the 1960s.

As already mentioned, the electrification of

Found in the back of an old picture frame, this photograph depicts wartime 'Austerity' Class No 90161 working an up goods past Northampton No 2 signal box. It is undated but is no later than 1967.

Author's collection

the West Coast Main Line (WCML) included the Northampton Loop. The Rugby–Euston main line was completed by 6 November 1965 and the loop line on 22 November.

Kilsby & Crick and Althorp Park stations closed in 1960, while Roade managed to survive until September 1964.

With the advent of the modernisation of the railways, the powers that be decided that Northampton needed a station that would reflect this image. It is claimed that an idea doodled on a bit of scrap paper went on to become the design for the new station – namely three concrete cowsheds bolted together – and it duly opened in 1966. The large goods sheds that had been built on the castle site were demolished to create more car-parking spaces. The town's population had continued to grow and with it a corresponding rise in commuters; in 1975 the population was 140,000, but by 2005 had risen to 192,000.

In September 1999 a new railfreight depot was opened north of Kilsby by the Tibbett & Britten Group and known as DIRFT (Daventry International Rail Freight Terminal). Why 'Daventry' is used in the title is not known, since the site is nowhere near

Daventry and is, in fact, much closer to Rugby! Although much of the railway's traditional freight traffic has disappeared, a lot of what is now carried is in the form of containers, and this type of traffic has increased as a result of the opening of the Channel Tunnel, coupled with the decline of much of Britain's manufacturing base. The result is that more and more manufactured goods are imported from Europe and, increasingly, China.

Sadly, the advent of privatisation has not done much for Northampton's travellers. Towards the end of 2004 the town found itself with two companies starting and terminating their services at Northampton. Whereas 'Silverlink County' ran through services from London to Birmingham, it now just runs between London and Northampton, with a 30-minute-interval service for most of the day. Central Trains now runs services between Northampton and Birmingham with an hourly service. This means that passengers to and from Long Buckby have to change at Northampton for London. One could be forgiven for thinking that someone, somewhere, doesn't like Northampton!

Above Northampton Castle station, obviously at the time of the introduction of the new electric services. *Author's collection*

Below Castle station in August 2006, showing the 'three concrete sheds bolted together'. *Author*

ENTER THE MIDLAND

While the London & North Western Railway (LNWR) – formed in 1846 by the amalgamation of the London & Birmingham Railway, the Grand Junction Railway and the Manchester & Birmingham Railway – was busy expanding its empire, it was not doing so in isolation. All over the country various groups were coming to realise that these newfangled railways had a huge potential – they could carry heavy goods, mainly coal from the mines to the expanding industrial areas, more cheaply and more quickly than the existing canals. They also had a potential for carrying passengers.

The Midland Railway (MR) was formed by the amalgamation of three companies on 10 May 1844, but before we move on from that date, and its effect on the county, it would be worthwhile to go back in time and look at how events led to the formation of this new company.

The Industrial Revolution could be said to have started at the beginning of the 18th century and to have developed rapidly over the next 100 years. Industry needed power, and the introduction of steam power meant that increasing amounts of coal were needed, which could only be carried by horse and cart or by river transport. In 1759 the Canal Act was passed by Parliament, leading to the creation of a national network of canals such that by 1830 some 4,000 miles had been built. Thus there came into existence a means of carrying large amounts of coal and goods quite easily, albeit at a slow speed and with limitations as to where it could go.

In earlier times, because of the difficulties of transporting coal, the mines tended to supply only the immediate area. However, the advent of the new canals, and in some cases the conversion of rivers into canals, meant that coal could be carried much further afield. Until the canal age Leicester, for many years an important manufacturing and commercial centre, was supplied with coal from the mines of North Leicestershire, based around the Moira and Coalville area, and received it by the old method of horse and cart.

With the conversion of the River Soar being pushed south from Loughborough, the mine-owners of North Leicestershire realised that, once the canal reached Leicester, the way would be clear for coal from the Trent coalfields to reach the city, and that it would, in all probability, be cheaper! They therefore began a strong and vociferous campaign to Parliament to stop it. In the end a compromise was reached. The canal would be built to Leicester, but an additional canal would be built westwards from the city towards the Leicestershire coalfields. This would enable the mine-owners to compete with one another, on a reasonably level playing-field.

October 1794 saw the official opening of the two canals. Competition, as expected, was fierce, but during the winter of 1798/99 an unforeseen blow was dealt to the Leicestershire mine-owners. In these days of mild winters it is difficult to appreciate how severe winters could be in the past. During that fateful winter a heavy snowfall followed by a rapid thaw saw not only parts of the Charnwood Forest Canal (the title given to the new canal extension westwards from Leicester) breached but also the canal's reservoir. The Leicestershire mine-owners, almost at a stroke, lost their transport system and were quickly in trouble. Naturally, their rivals lost no time in making good the coal previously supplied from the Leicestershire mines.

Canal-owners throughout the country faced no competition for nearly 30 years. Then early in the new century news spread of a new steam-powered locomotive that had been built by a Richard Trevithick in 1801. By 1808 he was in a position to be able to give a demonstration close to where Euston station stands today. This little single-cylinder locomotive was able to pull wagons round a circular track with curious members of the public paying 1 shilling for a ride The age of the railway, as we know it today, had arrived. By September 1825 the famous Stockton & Darlington Railway had opened, followed five years later, in September 1830, by the Liverpool & Manchester Railway.

In 1828 William Stenson, a partner in one of the Leicestershire coal mines, visited the Stockton & Darlington Railway; he saw what was going on there and realised that if there was a railway from his coal mines to Leicester, he could break the stranglehold held by the canal-owners in the Leicester area. Back home Stenson lost no time in convening a meeting of local mine-owners and industrialists. Among those gathering at the Bell Hotel in Leicester in February 1829 were the famous father and son George and Robert Stephenson, who had been invited in order to share their valuable experience of

Midland Railway, opened in May 1857 (distances from London St Pancras).

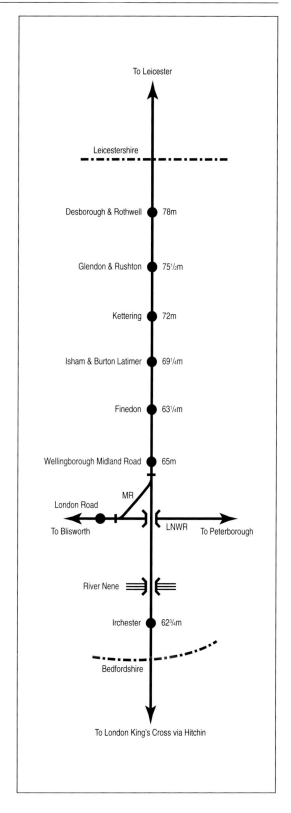

railway constriction. Another attender was John Ellis, a local landowner, businessman and Quaker.

The early days of the railways in Britain are full of references to the involvement of Quakers. Because of their strongly held religious beliefs, they had been denied entry to the major universities and had consequently turned their attention to the rapidly rising manufacturing industries. Their honesty in matters of business and finance meant that they could he trusted; in fact, many of today's well-known banks were started by Quakers. Therefore, if you were starting a new venture or business, having a Quaker on the committee usually meant that people would be willing to invest their money, which was why John Ellis was invited to this initial meeting, the outcome of which was a decision to build a railway from Leicester to Swannington. Despite a few difficulties, the line was fully open by November 1833.

With the railway up and running, the mine-owners of Nottinghamshire and the Trent Valley found themselves at a disadvantage. Coal was pouring into Leicester more cheaply than the canal-borne coal from the north. Indeed, even before the Leicester & Swannington Railway was fully open the Nottinghamshire mine-owners were meeting and deciding what action they should take. The answer was simply, if you can't beat 'em, join 'em!

At their meeting at the Sun Inn in Eastwood on 16 August 1832 they took the momentous decision to build a railway from their collieries to Leicester. Within weeks funding was forthcoming, and the title given to the proposed railway was to be the Midland Counties Railway (MCR), and it would connect Derby, Nottingham and Leicester and with London! Note how quickly what was originally intended to be a very provincial railway was changing and setting its sights on the capital! To reach London, the plan was to carry the line onwards from Leicester to Rugby and to connect with the London & Birmingham Railway (L&B).

Once news of this proposed route reached Northampton, a request was made to the MCR by the businessmen of that town – instead of joining the London & Birmingham at Rugby, why not come through Northampton via Market Harborough and proceed south of Northampton to join the L&B either at Blisworth or Roade? However, that route would involve crossing the Northamptonshire uplands and the Nene Valley and would have meant a significant increase in construction costs. After due consideration, the MCR took the decision to keep to the original plan and make the junction with the L&B at Rugby. For the second time Northampton had missed a main line to London.

The headquarters of the MCR was at Derby, and the first section of the railway opened in June 1839 between Derby and Nottingham. At Trent, which is roughly halfway between Derby and Nottingham, the line turned southwards. By May 1840 the line had reached Leicester, and was open to Rugby a month later. In August of that year another railway company, the Birmingham & Derby Junction Railway (B&DJR), opened its line from Derby to Hampton-in-Arden on the London & Birmingham line, and immediately offered an alternative route to London. In the years that followed these two companies were to spend much time and money in competing with each other for London traffic. Derby was to see a third company arrive on its doorstep with the arrival of the North Midland Railway (NMR), with a route from Derby to Masborough and Leeds, in May 1840.

Another famous name was appearing on the railway scene by now and was involved with, among many others, the NMR. This was George Hudson, born in 1800 at Howsham in the East Riding of Yorkshire. At the age of 27 Hudson inherited from his great uncle no less than £30,000, which by today's standards would be equal to several millions! From that moment his life changed dramatically, and his influence on the burgeoning railway scene was to be immense. Sadly, throughout his business life Hudson's name was to be associated with some dubious practices and shady dealings. Having said that, it must be admitted that he was a visionary and some of his schemes were good, and would certainly benefit Northamptonshire.

By 1842 the NMR was in financial difficulties and Hudson, never one to miss an opportunity, moved in and effectively took it over. He was quick to realise that if he could persuade the railway companies that met at Derby to amalgamate, not only would it put a stop to the competition between the MCR and the B&DJR for the London traffic, but it could enable Hudson to extend his activities southwards. Hudson therefore worked on the three companies until they agreed to merge. In May 1844 Parliament passed the Midland Amalgamation Bill, and on 24 May of that year the first committee meeting of the newly formed Midland Railway Company (MR) met and elected George Hudson as its first Chairman, with John Ellis, who was by now a Director of the MCR, as Deputy Chairman.

Hudson did not allow too much time to elapse before making plans to enlarge his business. Other railways were being built that would threaten his empire: one was the Leicester & Bedford, while another was the Northampton & Leicester Railway, also known as the South Midland. The Northampton line would have started either from a point on the L&B near Roade or from that company's Peterborough branch at Northampton itself, and would have proceeded to Leicester via Market Harborough.

Another player now moved on to the stage in the form of the Great Northern Railway (GNR), which was building a line from London King's Cross to York via Hitchin. The GNR began to show an interest in the Leicester & Bedford; if it could buy the line it would be able to make inroads into MR territory. Then to add to Hudson's worries, the Leicester & Bedford Railway re-registered itself and added a proposal to extend beyond Bedford to Hitchin. Much wheeling and dealing by Hudson resulted in a meeting in October 1846 between himself, Captain Law of the GNR and William Whitbread, a Bedfordshire landowner who was involved with the Leicester & Bedford scheme. The outcome was that the South Midland plan was dropped and the MR would buy the Leicester & Hitchin. One of the stipulations was that the line must be built within two years; however, this did not happen and time passed until 1852, when the originators of the Leicester & Bedford group went to Derby and demanded to know when their railway was going to be built.

This seems to have spurred on John Ellis, because within a year a Bill had been presented to Parliament and on 4 August 1853 the Leicester & Hitchin Act was passed. The route would start at Wigston, south of Leicester, and proceed through Market Harborough, Kettering, Wellingborough and Bedford to Hitchin. An agreement with the GNR would allow MR trains to travel over that company's line from Hitchin to King's Cross. Once the line was open, Midland trains would no longer need to travel over the LNWR to Euston.

One of the problems of using another company's tracks was that the host's trains were always given preference. The Midland had suffered a great deal with delays to its trains to London over the LNWR tracks; now, although the distance to be covered was much shorter using the GNR line from

Left The low winter sunshine of November 1972 highlights part of the original 1857 viaduct over the River Nene between Wellingborough and Irchester. *Author*

Below The ridge-and-furrow glazed roofs of Kettering's station canopies can be seen in the distance of this July 1971 view of the station from the Station signal box. A Class 45 diesel sets out with an up train. *Author*

Right A similar roof is to be found at Wellingborough station, seen here in February 1983. This is the point from which a barrow rolled into the path of a down Manchester express on 2 September 1898, resulting in the derailment of the train and the death of six passengers. *Author*

Hitchin, the same problems soon arose once more.

Despite its differences with the LNWR, the MR was quite happy to enter into an arrangement with it at Market Harborough. For 17 years the MR ran over the LNWR lines in that area, and also used the LNWR station until a new joint station opened in September 1884.

At the time that the Hitchin line was being built, the MR's coffers were hardly overflowing. The construction work was being done at the time of the Crimean War; there was a shortage of labourers and the cost of construction materials was rising sharply. The result was that the line had to be built to a price, and the effect of that decision was to be felt until comparatively recent years. Instead of tunnelling through the two main ridges at Desborough and Sharnbrook, the line went over them, which involved fairly steep gradients. The only tunnel was at Warden in Bedfordshire, 882 yards long. To reduce the height that the trains would need to climb, deep cuttings were excavated at the tops of both Desborough and Sharnbrook banks, but even so it was still necessary to provide a siding on the up side near Wymington into which lumbering loaded coal trains could be shunted while passenger trains passed.

One of the larger structures to be built within the county was the viaduct at Wellingborough, where the line crosses the River Nene and its flood plain. This viaduct gave great problems to the builders; in September 1855 it was reported that the abutments at each end had been pushed forward due to the movement of the ground (although it was claimed that not a single brick had been displaced), and three of the principal arches had to be taken down. Despite all the problems, Thomas Brassey, the main contractor, pressed on until the great day arrived on 4 May 1857, and the line was officially opened.

The Midland adopted a distinctive architectural style for its stations, but used local building materials. The two main stations at Kettering and Wellingborough were graced with ridge-and-furrow glazed roofs over the platforms, both of which can still be seen at the present time, though the former was changed considerably in 2000 when lifts were installed on all platforms.

When the line opened the passenger service consisted of five trains on weekdays and two on Sundays. Of the weekday trains, three were semi-fast, while the remaining two stopped at all stations, as did the two on Sundays. Trials were also undertaken with slip coaches. The last coach of a fast train was disconnected and allowed to coast into the station; this was done by a member of staff who was required to judge when to disconnect the coach and to control the brakes so as to bring the coach to a stand in the station. Getting this wrong meant being stranded until a locomotive could be organised to pull the coach into the station. Slip coaches were introduced for Wellingborough (1862) and Kettering (1914).

Everywhere there were huge increases in traffic flows. The coal from the Nottinghamshire coalfields that had flowed to Leicester now continued south to supply the huge demands of the capital, which had, until the arrival of the railways, been supplied by sea, down the coast from the mines of North East England.

Like its rival the LNWR, the MR had to think about quadrupling its main line to London. An additional problem facing the MR was the fact that it still had to hand over its traffic to the GNR at Hitchin. The answer was to for it to build its own line to London, and the company duly applied to Parliament. The Act (Extension to London) was passed in 1863 and authorised the MR to build a new line from Bedford to London St Pancras. This 50-mile stretch of new line opened in July

BR Standard Class '9F' 2-10-0 No 92160 heads an up goods on the slow lines added when the route was quadrupled; it has just past Irchester Junction signal box in May 1958. *Jim Pope*

1868, and with it the MR moved from being a provincial organisation based in Derby to a major player in the railway world. This fact was demonstrated by changing all the mileposts on the system, which instead of being measured from Derby were now measured from London.

With the new line in operation, the need to quadruple became more important. In Northamptonshire the first move was the opening of the new line from Manton to Glendon via Corby in 1880. From Glendon southwards, work continued on the quadrupling, and by December 1883 the new

lines were in place between Wellingborough and Irchester and, as we shall see later, this paved the way for the Higham Ferrers branch to be built.

Wellingborough increasingly became an important centre, being roughly halfway between London and the coalfields of Nottinghamshire and Derbyshire. As a result a large locomotive depot was built, together with a hostel for the crews, who often needed overnight accommodation. Large marshalling yards were built in the Finedon Road area.

In what is believed to be one of the few photographs of Pytchley signal box, Johnson '1P' 2-4-0 No 266 has just come off the Huntingdon branch and is heading for Kettering. The date is unknown, but is pre-1934. The box opened in February 1906 and closed in April 1935. *Geoff Goslin collection*

Right A posed group of staff from the goods depot at Desborough & Rothwell station. Note the MR steam lorry and the dog carrying the basket. *Courtesy of Desborough Civic Society*

Left An early photograph of a train at Irchester: note the poor sighting of the signals by the staircase to the main buildings and the elegant hat worn by the lady leaning out of the carriage on the right. *David Tee collection*

Below Irchester station was unusual in that the station building was at right-angles to the tracks and above them at road level. It is seen here in April 1959. *H. C. Casserley*

With industry booming in the country, there was a corresponding rise in the iron and steel industries, with, as we have already noted, much of the raw material being quarried in Northamptonshire, and requiring transport to the various foundries and steel-producing plants, again many being sited in the county. Another, much smaller, locomotive depot was opened at Kettering in 1865 and was used to service the locomotives on the Huntingdon branch, which saved them having to run to Wellingborough. This depot closed in June 1965.

With the quadrupling complete and with its own line all the way to London, the MR continued its steady expansion. As well as Wellingborough and Kettering, smaller stations had been opened at Desborough & Rothwell, Glendon & Rushton, Isham & Burton Latimer, Finedon and Irchester.

For many people, the large-scale closure of many stations in the 1950s and '60s is seen as

A picture to evoke memories: An '8F', working hard, comes up the spur from Wellingborough (London Road) on to the Midland main line with, in all probability, a load of iron ore. The wartime replacement signal box at Wellingborough Junction is on the left.
J. D. Lyne

the start of the decline in railways, but history shows us that this process started much earlier. In July 1909 the MR announced the closure of some signal boxes on Sundays, followed in 1921 by the closure on Sundays of Finedon and Glendon & Rushton stations.

The Grouping of 1923 had little effect on the line, since it was all part of the old Midland Railway, the only exception being the connection at Wellingborough with the Peterborough branch of the LNWR, which of course also became part of the LMS. Likewise, with the nationalisation of the railways in 1948 there were no dramatic changes to the regime. However, unlike the West Coast Main Line (WCML) through the county, which was promised a programme of modernisation and electrification, no such plan was forthcoming for the Midland Main Line (MML). Indeed, in September 1967 British Railways (BR) announced plans to demolish St Pancras station; thankfully this came to nothing, and in December 1968, exactly 100 years since it opened, BR said that it would not be proceeding with this plan.

Closure of smaller stations had started in LMS days, with Finedon being the first to

Above A delightful shot of the driver of 'Peak' No 70 (later Class 45 No 45048) on a down express awaiting the 'right away' at Wellingborough in July 1972. *Author*

Below At one time there was a regular coach service between Kettering station and Peterborough. In June 1980 a coach is seen outside Kettering station. *Author*

A reminder that, for a short period in 2003, Wellingborough and Kettering saw through services to Manchester again while upgrading of the WCML was in progress. *Author*

close in December 1940 followed by Isham & Burton Latimer in November 1950, Glendon & Rushton in January 1960, Irchester in March 1960 and finally Desborough & Rothwell in January 1968.

The 1960s saw the demise of steam locomotives on the MML. In their place came diesel locomotives, the Class 45 'Peak' Class being the most commonly used. They were to be the mainstay of the great majority of passenger services until the advent of the High Speed Trains (HSTs), first introduced on the MML in 1982. These trains revolutionised the service, and in 2005 are still providing the majority of the long-distance services.

In the 1970s the MML between St Pancras and Bedford was electrified, and it was hoped that the electrification programme would be extended northwards. Sadly this came to naught. However, the advent of privatisation in the 1990s brought a level of service to the MML that is better that at any time in its history. The company that won the franchise was appropriately named 'Midland Mainline', and one of its first innovations was to introduce, in 1998, the 'Turbostars'. These were a new generation of DMUs that were faster and smoother-riding compared to some earlier classes. With these in service, Midland Mainline introduced a new timetable that gave a 30-minute-frequency service in both directions for Wellingborough and Kettering, with the HSTs continuing to operate the longer journeys. Despite the frequency of trains there were still instances of overcrowding on the morning commuter trains to London; between 0500 and 0900 the current timetable shows 11 trains to London. Such is the popularity of the route that some commuters from Northampton prefer to drive to Wellingborough in order to reach London.

When introduced, the 'Turbostars' were only two-car units, but to help with the overcrowding a third coach was introduced. At the end of 2004 the 'Turbostars' were gradually replaced by a new generation of DMUs. The 'Meridians' are four-car DMUs, and have not only helped with the overcrowding, but are also proving to be capable of higher speeds than the 'Turbostars'. As to the future, with St Pancras becoming the main station for the European services, one can see the day when, with one change of train, Paris and Brussels will only be a few hours from Kettering and Wellingborough.

Stratford-upon-Avon & Midland Junction Railway

It has been said on more than one occasion that Northamptonshire is the county that one travels *through*, either by road or rail, to reach one's destination. Of the four main lines that passed through the county, not one had its origins within it. There was, however, a fifth railway company that was different. Not only did it have Northampton as part of its title, but much of its mileage was within the county; moreover, and just to be different from the others, its lines went in a roughly east to west direction, rather than south to north.

The question that is usually asked is why would anyone want to build a railway that ran through what was, and still is, a sparsely populated part of the county? The answer lay in what had been found in large quantities throughout the county – iron ore.

By 1825 there were well over 300 furnaces in the UK, many in South Wales where there were, at the outset, ample supplies of the main materials needed for the production of iron – coal and iron ore. Such was the growth of the industry that the local supplies of iron ore, which were not of the best quality, were rapidly becoming depleted, and new supplies were urgently required.

Railway entrepreneurs were not slow to realise that if there was a more direct rail route from the iron-ore-producing areas of Northamptonshire to the existing network of railways to the west, the iron ore could be transported more quickly and the scheme would be financially viable.

What was to become the Stratford-upon-Avon & Midland Junction Railway (SMJ) did not come into existence in its final form until 1910. More than 50 years had passed since the first player moved on to the stage, and during that period the raison d'être for the proposed lines had gone, and cheaper iron ore was being imported from Spain. How the different companies that subsequently became the SMJ managed to survive in any form for so long is little short of miraculous. But survive they did, and the history of those 50 years, while somewhat complicated, is a vital part of the county's railway history and gives an insight as to how the investors were willing to keep pressing on, despite all the problems they encountered.

The first company on the scene was the Northampton & Banbury Railway (N&BR), which obtained its Act in July 1847. This gave it the authority to build a line from a junction with the Northampton-Peterborough branch of the LNWR near Northampton, crossing the LNWR line at Blisworth, then proceeding westward via Towcester, finally to make a junction with the Buckinghamshire Railway at a remote spot called Cockley Brake, roughly midway between Greatworth and Farthinghoe. From there the N&BR had running powers to Banbury. This is one of many examples where the places mentioned in the titles were never actually reached directly by the company!

Not much happened for some time. The LNWR agreed to build the line and to have it

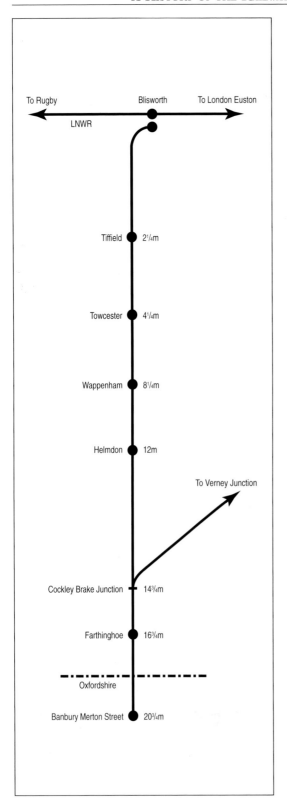

To Rugby   Blisworth   To London Euston

LNWR

Tiffield   2¼m

Towcester   4¼m

Wappenham   8¼m

Helmdon   12m

To Verney Junction

Cockley Brake Junction   14¾m

Farthinghoe   16¾m

Oxfordshire

Banbury Merton Street   20¾m

completed in five years, but again nothing happened during that period, something that will be encountered several times as the story unfolds. In July 1863 a new Act was proposed and obtained. The name of the company now had the word 'Junction' added, so the Northampton & Banbury Junction Railway (N&BJR) came into existence. The principal difference from the original route was that instead of starting near Northampton, it would start at Blisworth, which would make its title even more inaccurate. The Act also gave the N&BJR running powers over the LNWR from Blisworth to Northampton, although it is uncertain if they ever exercised their right.

It was not until May 1866 that the first section of line opened between Blisworth and Towcester. Nearly 20 years had elapsed since the company had obtained its Act, and all it had managed was the building of just over 4 miles of track! At Blisworth the N&BJR built its station adjacent to that of the LNWR, with a subway linking the two. There was no direct rail connection between the LNWR and the N&BJR, all movements having to go through exchange sidings. Continuing in a south-westerly direction, there was just one station between Blisworth and Towcester, at Tiffield, which was little more than a wooden platform and only had a life of two years, between 1869 and 1871.

Flushed with this 'success', the company changed its name again in July 1866 to the Midland Counties & South Wales Railway. In July 1870, with no more of its lines open or even built, the company changed its name back to the N&BJR.

By August 1871 the line had been extended from Towcester to Helmdon, though initially this was for goods only. Almost another year was to pass before the line finally reached Cockley Brake Junction. Through services started, eventually, on 1 June

Northampton & Banbury Junction Railway, opened throughout in June 1872 (distances from Blisworth).

Above Cockley Brake Junction signal box in March 1955: a recent visit to the site uncovered various artefacts. *R. M. Casserley*

Below Banbury (Merton Street) in March 1960, with a railcar for Buckingham. *F. G. Cockman*

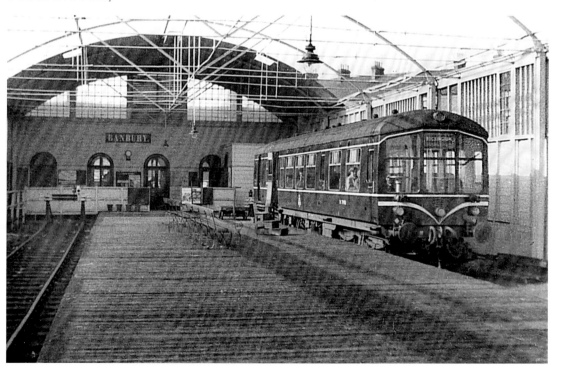

Above **The SMJ at Blisworth: Class '4F' No 44567 waits with a train for Stratford in April 1952. The LNWR lines are off to the left.** *R. M. Casserley*

Below **The SMJ built three cottages at Blisworth for its staff. Note the 'SMJ' and '1914' stones set into the brickwork, photographed in March 2000.** *Author*

1872. In November 1876 the LNWR took over the running of the line, despite having failed to complete its building within the five years stipulated in the original Act.

With the first half of what was to become the SMJ up and running, we can turn our attention to the other half, namely the East & West Junction Railway.

Above Towcester station, looking towards Blisworth in April 1956. *R. M. Casserley*

Above The exterior of Towcester station in April 1965. *R. M. Casserley*

Below A Northampton & Banbury Junction timetable for March 1873. *Author's collection*

NORTHAMPTON & BANBURY JUNCTION.

	WEEK DAYS ONLY.										WEEK DAYS ONLY.							
	Parl.	1,2,3,	1,2,3,	1,2,3,	1,2,3,	1,2,3,					Parl.	1,2,3,	1,2,3.	1,2,3.	1,2,3,		
	a m	a m	a m	p m	p m	p m					a m	a m	p m	p m	p m		
North'ton ..dep.	8 10	—	10 40	2 5	4 15	7 13	—	—	Banbury ....dep.	7 14	10 5	11 4	3 3	6 39	—	—
Blisworth	8 30	—	11 38	2 30	4 40	7 45	—	—	Farthinghoe......	7 21	10 12	11 50	3 10	6 37	—	—
Towcester	8 40	—	11 48	3 0	4 50	7 55	—	—	Helmdon	7 36	10 27	12 13	3 25	6 52	—	—
Wappenham	8 50	—	11 58	3 12	5 0	8 5	—	—	Wappenham	7 44	10 37	12 33	3 35	7 2	—	—
Helmdon	8 58	—	12 8	3 35	5 8	8 15	—	—	Towcester........	7 51	10 45	1 3	3 45	7 12	—	—
Farthinghoe......	9 12	—	12 23	3 55	5 22	8 30	—	—	Blisworth	9 15	11 35	1 45	4 20	7 45	—	—
Banbury ......arr.	9 24	—	12 35	4 10	5 34	8 42	—	—	North'ton .. arr.	9 25	11 45	1 55	4 30	7 55	—	—

The Classes shown above refer only to trains between Towcester and Banbury.

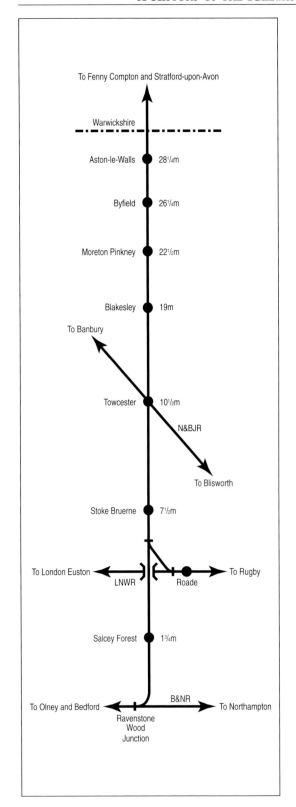

To Fenny Compton and Stratford-upon-Avon

Warwickshire

Aston-le-Walls — 28¼m

Byfield — 26¼m

Moreton Pinkney — 22½m

Blakesley — 19m

To Banbury

Towcester — 10½m

N&BJR

To Blisworth

Stoke Bruerne — 7½m

To London Euston ← | LNWR | • Roade → To Rugby

Salcey Forest — 1¾m

B&NR
To Olney and Bedford ← Ravenstone Wood Junction → To Northampton

East & West Junction Railway

The history of this part of the SMJ is complicated, and to try and make it as readable as possible I have tried a 'timeline' approach.

June 1864

The East & West Junction Railway (E&WJR) received the Royal Assent. The line would run from a junction with the N&BJR at Greens Norton, 2 miles west of Towcester, to a junction with the Great Western Railway at Old Stratford, a distance of 33¼ miles. The company was also granted the right to run its own trains over the N&BJR from Towcester to Blisworth.

August 1864

Work on the line was started at Towcester, with Viscountess Palmerston cutting the first sod. In 1866 powers were granted to allow the company to raise up to £400,000 in order to allow work on the line to continue and to make it double track. However, the company failed to raise the money and work was consequently suspended.

July 1869

The company reached an agreement with its creditors that enabled work to be restarted, *but* with the proviso that it must be completed within two years and total costs must not exceed £230,000.

June 1871

The first section of the line opened between Fenny Compton and Kineton, with an exchange siding with the GWR at Fenny Compton. This was the only section of the line that was completed within the time limit set in 1869. Later that year the company was granted a further three years to complete the work.

East & West Junction Railway: Towcester–Fenny Compton opened in July 1873, Towcester–Ravenstone Wood Junction in December 1892 (distances from Ravenstone Wood Junction).

July 1873

The remaining two sections of line were opened, from Stratford-upon-Avon to Kineton and Fenny Compton to Greens Norton. With the line now complete, the LNWR introduced a Euston to Stratford-upon-Avon service.

August 1873

Despite the parlous state of its finances, the company put forward proposals to extend its line westward from Stratford! Amazingly, Parliament granted powers for the Evesham, Redditch & Stratford-upon-Avon Junction Railway (ER&SJR). This new line, some 7¾ miles long, started at Stratford and went westward to make a junction with the Evesham & Redditch Railway at Broom. This latter company was to become part of the Midland Railway in 1882.

January 1875

With debts rising and its credit overstretched, a receiver was appointed by the Chancery Court.

July 1877

All passenger services were suspended and remained so for the next eight years.

June 1879

The ER&SJR opened for traffic. This part of the E&WR was not subject to the suspension in force on the rest of the system. With its finances in a worse position than in August 1873, the company applied to Parliament for the right to extend eastwards from Towcester! The new proposed company had the long-winded title of the Easton Neston Mineral & Towcester, Roade & Olney Junction Railway (ENM&TR&OJR) – but at least it was an accurate description of where the planned line was to start and finish. The 10½-mile line would start at Towcester and make a junction with the Bedford & Northampton Railway (B&NR) at Ravenstone Wood Junction, some 4 miles west of Olney. The B&NR had opened in 1872 and became part of the MR in 1885.

August 1882

The ENM&TR&OJR was close to being abandoned – all it succeeded in doing was to change its name to the Stratford-upon-Avon, Towcester & Midland Junction Railway (ST&MJR).

March 1885

Passenger services were restored between Blisworth and Broom.

January 1886

The ER&SJR failed, and was put into receivership.

December 1887

The first sod of the ST&MJR was cut at Towcester by Sir Thomas Hesketh. By this time the company had reached an agreement with the N&BJ in 1883 to use its station at Towcester. Almost immediately the company found itself in financial difficulties and work on the line stopped. Authority was given for the work to continue, but with a two-year deadline. In 1889 a further two-year extension was granted.

April 1889

The ST&MJR made an agreement with the MR whereby its trains could run over the MR to Olney from the junction at Ravenstone Wood.

April 1891

The ST&MJR opened, albeit for goods traffic only. With the MR at both ends of its system, that company started to run the trains throughout. At Roade, where the line crossed the West Coast Main Line just to the south of the LNWR station, a west-to-north connection was built to link the two lines. An extra platform was built at the LNWR station for what was hoped would be a Roade to Towcester service, but this never started; the connection saw little use and was closed in May

Stoke Bruerne station. *From a painting by Barry Taylor*

1917. Between Towcester and Ravenstone, two stations were opened, at Stoke Bruerne and Salcey Forest. The latter could only be reached by crossing fields, and both were in remote parts of the county, thus generating little or no revenue. With the financial problems facing the company, it is difficult to understand why it constructed such substantial buildings (that at Stoke Bruerne is still there for all to see). Both opened in December 1892 and were closed in April 1893, a life of four months.

May 1898

The ST&MJR failed, and joined the ER&SJR and the E&WJR in receivership. An Act of Parliament was obtained that would allow the three companies, now referred to as the Midland Counties Junction Railway, to be sold as a job lot! Neither the MR, the GWR at Stratford and Fenny Compton, nor the LNWR at Blisworth and Roade was interested. By this time the Great Central Railway (GCR) had swept through the county, but again it were not interested.

September 1908

The Joint Committee presented a Bill to Parliament for the amalgamation of all three companies to form the Stratford-upon-Avon & Midland Junction Railway (SMJ), which was passed. The Act also gave the MR and the GCR running rights over the entire system,

while the GWR was only given the right to run between Stratford and Fenny Compton. The LNWR was given running rights between Roade and Stratford.

January 1909

The SMJ came into existence and quickly started negotiations with the N&BJR, which, like the others, was in financial trouble. In April 1910 Parliament passed an Act that allowed the merger, and the SMJ, as most people know it, had arrived. It was an incredible tale of endurance in the face of the financial difficulties that had plagued the different companies from the very beginning.

The SMJ

With the merger complete, the new management could start to take decisions that would not only improve its services to the general public but also, by the removal of the competitive factor, start to make savings on the operational front. For example, as already stated, although the passenger services had always been sparse, there would now only need to be one service running between Towcester and Blisworth. Another saving was the decision to remove the junction and signal box at Greens Norton; the two single lines, one from Banbury and the other from

Stratford, would continue separately to Towcester station, where, if necessary, trains could cross. At the same time, its was also decided to do away with the two signal boxes at Towcester, where previously there had been one at each end of the station, and a new box was built at the north-east end. On a small system such as the SMJ, the savings achieved by this rationalisation would be quite significant.

The management of the new company, under the Chairmanship of Harry Willmott (who had been chairman of the E&WJR since 1907), together with some of the local landowners and gentry who sat on the Board, began to see the potential of new traffic in the form of tourism.

American visitors were beginning to take a very active interest in two places that came within the catchment area of the SMJ, Stratford-upon-Avon, with its Shakespearean connections, and Sulgrave Manor, with its direct link with America's first President, George Washington – in later years the SMJ was to be known as 'The Shakespeare Route'. When the Northampton to Bedford line opened in June 1872, it was possible to run through trains from St Pancras via Bedford direct to Stratford, making connection with the SMJ at Ravenstone Wood Junction. Towards the other end of the system, the Great Central, which had opened through the county in 1899, made two connections with the SMJ near Byfield – one a north-to-west spur and the other south-to-west – which

meant that it was now possible to run through trains to Stratford via the Great Central. The south-to-west curve only had a very short life, being closed in 1900.

In 1910, following petitions from local people, the SMJ opened a small siding with a platform for goods only at Aston-le-Walls; this was some 2 miles west of Byfield, where the Aston-le-Walls to Boddington road crossed the railway, and it remained open until January 1953. Some years ago someone writing about the SMJ stated that, 'Nothing remains to be seen…' Well, despite so much of the SMJ having disappeared completely, Aston le Walls was still there amongst the vegetation in 2002, and there is more, providing one is prepared to go and look for it.

An innovation pioneered by the SMJ was the 'Railophone' apparatus. Although these days the mobile phone is commonplace, in 1911 both the telephone and the wireless were still quite a novelty. Imagine being able to make a telephone call from a moving train! Invented by a German, Herr Von Kramer, it had been tried on another railway before the SMJ decided to have a test section fitted with the equipment. Some 9 miles between Stratford and Kineton was chosen, and on 20 April 1911 the Mayor of Stratford, travelling on the train, spoke to a local writer, Miss Marie Corelli. The novelty value was, however, short-lived, but far more important was the realisation that this system could be used as a train control safety feature. It would be fair to say that what would become known as

A Stephenson Locomotive Society special at Byfield in April 1956 headed by Midland '3F' No 43222. Just visible above the water tank is a signal with an LNWR arm. Note that not one of the members roaming the track appears to be wearing an HV vest. Happy days!
R. M. Casserley

Automatic Train Control stemmed from these experiments. Perhaps its German inventor, together with the onset of the First World War, was the major reason for its demise.

Such were the improving finances of the company that by 1912 the Board was able to announce, perhaps for the first time in 50 years, that they would be able to pay a dividend. Doubtless some of this was due to the extra traffic being generated from the various ironstone mines that had been opened adjacent to the SMJ. In addition to the mines at Easton Neston, there were others in the Blisworth area, at Byfield, and, out of the county, at Edge Hill.

The years between the formation of the SMJ in 1909 and 1914 were perhaps, for many employees, the best years of the line's history. For several years during that period one of the principal Directors of the company, Lord Willoughby de Broke of Compton Verney, was in the habit of inviting all the staff to his home for an annual party. Quite who ran the railway on these days is not known. There is no doubt that the company did adopt quite a paternalistic attitude to its staff; with a total staff of about 250, it was possible for a family atmosphere to exist.

Sadly the advent of the Great War would bring this to an end. During that conflict 60 of the men were called up for military service, seven of them dying in action.

The SMJ in LMS days

After the Grouping in 1923, one of the first things the LMS did was to re-lay the trackwork on various parts of the old SMJ, enabling more powerful locomotives to work over the system. Apart from normal passenger services and the daily pick-up goods trains that worked through the area, one of the more unusual traffic flows was the banana trains. These started their journey at Avonmouth Docks and came up through Gloucester, Ashchurch and Broom; at the latter place it was necessary for the trains to reverse in order to access the SMJ. Once on the SMJ they were routed via Olney and Bedford to Somers Town (St Pancras) in London, where Fyffes had its principal depot. This gave the LMS an advantage over the GWR – its biggest competitor – for the banana traffic, since the Great Western had no direct connection to Fyffe's at Somers Town.

Banana traffic was, unlike today, a seasonal traffic, and in consequence it was important that these trains had a clear run whenever possible. The SMJ portion, being single track, required special planning to make sure that this was achieved. With all the route now part of the LMS it became possible for train crews to work over the old SMJ and MR routes without the necessity to change crews at Olney and Stratford.

The LMS was fully aware of the London-Stratford tourist traffic and set about capturing it, being again in direct competition with the GWR and its route via Oxford and Banbury. One of its moves was to buy a large house near Stratford and convert it into a hotel, naming it, appropriately enough, the Welcombe Hotel. This opened its doors to the public in 1931. A year later another novelty was tried on the line from Blisworth to Stratford, in the form of a single-deck bus that had both rubber wheels for running on a road and a set of flanged wheels that enabled it run on the railway. The principal selling point was that passengers only had to change at Blisworth, because the train, once at Stratford, could drive off the railway tracks and go straight up to the hotel. Built by Karrier Motors of Huddersfield, it was known as the 'Ro Railer'.

During my researches for this book, I was fortunate to meet a gentleman who had actually travelled on it. He had been to Stratford by the normal service and had seen this conveyance making its way to the hotel. His return journey to Blisworth coincided with the return journey of the Ro Railer. Let me quote from his letter:

'It soon returned from the hotel, straddled the rail track in a siding, lowered its rail wheels and raised its road wheels. It then moved into the station platform and I entrained for a fast, but ear-shattering journey back to Blisworth, calling only at Towcester. This service did not last very long.'

How true. The experiment started in April 1932 and finished in June of the same year, when the service reverted to conventional methods.

The nationalisation of the railways in 1948 made little difference initially. Then, in 1953, the railways were reorganised and the old SMJ found itself part of the London Midland Region at its eastern end and the Western Region at its western end. This arrangement did not work too well and, despite an increase in freight traffic, particularly between Broom and Woodford Halse, it was the beginning of the end for the SMJ.

Closure of stations to passenger services started with Helmdon and Wappenham in July 1951. Towcester, Blakesley, Morton Pinkney and Byfield followed in April 1952, with Byfield hanging on until November of that year.

Gradually the remaining freight traffic was re-routed, and by the end of the 1950s the SMJ in Northamptonshire was completely closed. The part of the E&WJR between Fenny Compton was handed over to the MOD, and is still in situ.

Before we leave the SMJ, readers may care to share my memories of the only journey I made over part of the system.

It must have been some time in the late 1940s. My favourite aunt lived in Rushden and for many years there was a gathering of the Butler side of the family at Christmas. Part of the celebrations always included a Christmas tree festooned with presents. I recall one occasion when I noticed that my present appeared to be little more than an envelope. My heart sank. Such a small present!

Christmas Day came and, on opening the envelope, I found a letter from my aunt asking if I would like to go with her to visit her brother, my uncle, at Kineton. Uncle Eric, or, to give him his full title, Rev Eric Boyce Butler, was the Methodist minister at Kineton and, probably because of his duties, had not been able to join the family gathering. The letter said that since we would need to make an early start I would need to spend the previous night at my aunt's.

Although I was by then quite a seasoned rail traveller, having lived with my parents first in Portsmouth, then just outside Oban in Scotland for much of the war years, I was delighted at the prospect of this journey.

The morning we travelled was, I remember, clear with a sharp frost, and we walked and slid our way down Midland Road and Station Road in Rushden to the station. Our journey is shown in the table.

Four different trains for only 49 rail miles! Nevertheless, they dovetailed well. Our return journey in the evening was completed in about the same time and with good connections throughout. Little did I realise at the time what a unique opportunity this was. Thank you, aunt, for that unusual Christmas gift.

	arr	dep
Rushden		07.12
Wellingborough		
Midland Road	07.18	07.33
Northampton Castle	07.54	08.25
Blisworth	08.35	08.55
Kineton	10.06	

Table 199 WELLINGBORO' AND HIGHAM FERRERS

WEEKDAYS ONLY. Third Class Only

Miles		a.m.	a.m.	a.m.	a.m.	p.m.		p.m.	p.m.	p.m.	p.m.	p.m.	p.m.	p.m.	p.m.		
—	**WELLINGBORO'** (Mid. Rd.) .... dep.	6 40	7 55	8 45	9 45	1 0	...	3 42	5 5	5 47	6 25	7 5	8 2	9 17	9 56	...	...
3¾	Rushden	6 57	8 4	8 54	9 54	1 9	...	3 51	5 14	5 56	6 34	7 14	8 11	9 26	10 5	...	...
4¾	**HIGHAM FERRERS** .... arr.	7 0	8 7	8 57	9 57	1 12	...	3 54	5 17	5 59	6 37	7 17	8 14	9 29	10 8	...	...

Miles		a.m.	a.m.	a.m.	a.m.		p.m.	p.m.	p.m.	p.m.	p.m.	p.m.	p.m.	p.m.	p.m.		
—	**HIGHAM FERRERS** .... dep.	7 8	8 15	9 20	10 3	...	1 30	4 15	5 25	6 5	6 45	7 22	8 20	9 37	10 14	...	...
1	Rushden	7 12	8 19	9 24	10 7	...	1 34	4 19	5 29	6 9	6 49	7 26	8 24	9 41	10 18	...	...
4¾	**WELLINGBORO'** (Mid. Rd.) .... arr.	7 18	8 25	9 30	10 13	...	1 40	4 25	5 35	6 15	6 55	7 32	8 30	9 47	10 24	...	...

Table 198 WELLINGBORO' AND NORTHAMPTON

Miles		WEEKDAYS																SUNDAYS		
														TC	SO	TC				
		a.m.	a.m.	a.m.	a.m.	a.m.	a.m.	p.m.	p.m.	p.m.	p.m.	p.m.	p.m.	p.m.	p.m.	p.m.		a.m.	p.m.	p.m.
—	**WELLINGBORO' (M. Rd.)** dep.	7 32	...	8 45	...	...	11 15	...	1 55	3 50	...	5 40	...	8 0	...	10 5	...	10 20	9 28	10 30
1	„ **(L. Rd.)** ...	...	7 44	...	9 0	10 44	11 18	1 41	1 58	3 53	4 56	5 43	7 31	8 6	9 47	...	...	...	...	...
5	Castle Ashby & Earls Barton	...	7 52	...	9 8	10 51	...	1 48	2 6	...	5 2	...	...	8 14	...	...	...	...	...	...
8	Billing	...	7 58	...	9 14	10 57	...	1 54	...	...	5 8		7 43	...	...	...	...	...	...	...
12	**NORTHAMPTON (B. St.)**	...	8 5	...	9 22	11 5	11 38	2 2	2 18	4 11	5 16	6 1	7 51	8 27	10 5	...	...	...	...	...
13	„ **(Castle)** arr.	7B54	8 9	9 9	9 26	11 9	11 42	2 6	2 22	4 16	5 20	6 5	7 55	8 34	10 9	10 27	...	10 40	9 50	10 52

Miles		A SO	TC	SX			TC		TC	TC			SO	SX		SO				
		a.m.	a.m.	a.m.	a.m.	a.m.	a.m.	p.m.	p.m.	p.m.	p.m.	p.m.	p.m.	p.m.	p.m.	p.m.		a.m.	p.m.	p.m.
—	**NORTHAMPTON (Castle)** dep.	6 40	7 0	7 18	9 46	10 5	11 45	12 20	2 11	4 30	5 15	5 48	6 35	7 30	8 45	9 25	...	9 30	7 30	9 8
	(B. St.)	6 44	7 3	7 22	9 49	...	...	12 23	2 14	4 33	5 18	5SO51	6 38	7 33	...	9 28	...	...	...	...
5	Billing	6 51	...	7 29	9 56	...	...	12 30	2 21	...	5 25	...	6 45	7 40	...	...	...	...	...	...
8	Castle Ashby & Earls Barton	6 57	...	7 35	10 2	...	p.m.	...	...	...	5 31	6 2	6 51	7 46	...	...	...	...	...	...
12	**WELLINGBORO' (L. Rd.)** ...	7 6	...	7 44	10 10	10 23	12 3	12 45	2 34	4 51	5 43	6 12	7 2	7 57	9 5	9 47	...	...	...	...
13	„ **(M. Rd.)** arr.	...	7 22	...	...	10 27	12 7	...	2 39	4 55	...	6 16	...	...	9 9	...	...	9 50	7 50	9 28

SO—Saturdays only. **SX**—Saturdays excepted. **TC**—Through Carriages from or to Leicester. (Table 180.)
A—Conveys Through Carriages Commencing July 1st Northampton to Yarmouth (Table 61). **B**—On Saturdays arrives Northampton 7.56 a.m.

LEAMINGTON SPA, DAVENTRY, WEEDON BLISWORTH AND NORTHAMPTON

Miles.		WEEKDAYS ONLY																		
				B						SO										
		a.m.	a.m.	a.m.	a.m.	a.m.	a.m.	a.m.	a.m.	p.m.	p.m.	p.m.	p.m.	p.m.	p.m.	p.m.	p.m.	p.m.	p.m.	
0	Warwick (Milverton) ......dep.	.	6 37	7 5	.	.	.	.	.	12 43	.	.	.	2 52	.	4 16	.	6 9	.	.
¾	**Leamington Spa**............ „	...	6 47	7 30	...	...	...	...	...	12 51	...	...	...	2 58	...	4 25	...	6 30	...	...
8	Southam & Long I.	.	7 2	7 45	.	.	.	.	.	1 6	.	.	.	3 13	.	4 40	.	6 45	.	.
10	Napton & Stockton	...	7 8	7 51	...	...	...	...	...	1 12	...	...	...	3 19	...	4 46	...	6 51	...	...
13¼	Flecknoe............................	.	7 15	.	.	.	.	.	.	.	.	.	.	3 26	.	.	.	6 58	.	.
16	Braunston	...	7 22	...	...	...	...	...	...	...	...	...	...	3 33	...	...	...	7 5	...	...
19¼	Daventry...................... arr.	.	7 30	.	.	.	.	.	.	.	.	.	.	3 41	.	.	.	7 13	.	.
	dep.	...	7 32	...	...	...	...	...	...	...	...	...	...	3 43	...	...	...	7 23	...	...
23¼	**Weedon** .... arr.	.	7 44	.	.	.	.	.	.	.	.	.	.	3 52	.	.	.	7 36	.	.
30¼	Blisworth .... arr.	...	7 56	...	...	...	...	...	...	...	...	...	...	4 3	...	...	...	7 48	...	...
	dep.	6 54	.	.	8 45	9 25	10 1	10 20	11 45	.	12 40	1 53	3 5	4 14	5 58	.	7 35	8 10	10 5	.
35	**Northampton** (Castle) ... arr.	7 5	...	...	8 55	9 35	10 11	10 30	11 55	...	12 50	2 3	3 15	4 24	6 8	...	7 45	8 20	10 15	...
100¼	**London** (Euston) .... arr.	.	9 44	.	.	.	.	.	.	.	.	.	.	7 45	.	.	.	10C54	.	.

For Notes see Page 185.

STRATFORD-ON-AVON, BANBURY AND BLISWORTH

THIRD CLASS ONLY

		WEEKDAYS ONLY					
				SO	SX		
		a.m.	a.m.	a.m.	p.m.	p.m.	p.m.
—	**STRATFORD-ON-AVON** dep.	7 12	...	11 58	...	...	6 40
5½	Ettington	7 24	...	12 11	...	...	6 53
9½	Kineton	7 32	...	12 19	...	...	7 1
15¾	Fenny Compton....................	7 46	...	12 33	...	...	7 13
22½	Byfield	7 59	...	12 46	4 45	...	7 26
26¾	Morton Pinkney....................	8 8	...	12 56	4 55	...	7 36
29¾	Blakesley	8 15	...	1 3	5 1	...	7 44
—	**BANBURY** ....dep.	...	10 40	...	...	4 45	...
3¾	Farthinghoe	...	10 49	...	...	4 54	...
8½	Helmdon...............................	...	11 2	...	...	5 7	...
12¾	Wappenham	...	11 11	...	...	5 15	...
16½	Towcester	8 25	11 21	1 11	5 10	5 23	7 52
—	**BLISWORTH** ....arr.	8 36	11 30	1 22	5 20	5 32	8 2
½	50 **NORTHAMPTON**...........arr.	8 55	11 55	2 3	...	6 8	8 20
½	50 **LONDON (Euston)**.........arr.	10 21	3c41	4 15	...	7 45	10 57

		WEEKDAYS ONLY					
				SO	SX		
		a.m.	a.m.	a.m.	a.m.	p.m.	p.m.
—	50 **LONDON (Euston)** ......dep.	6 40	...	11 32	11 32	4 35	...
—	50 **NORTHAMPTON**	8 25	9 0	1 30	2 32	5 30	6 14
—	**BLISWORTH** ....dep.	8 55	9 31	2 0	4 0	6 0	6 50
4	Towcester	9A10	9 41	2 10	4B15	6 10	7 0
8	Wappenham	...	9 51	...	...	6 22	...
11½	Helmdon...............................	...	10 0	...	...	6 32	...
16½	Farthinghoe	...	10 12	...	...	6 47	...
20½	**BANBURY** ....arr.	...	10 20	...	...	6 55	...
8½	Blakesley	9 17	...	2 19	4 23	...	7 7
11½	Morton Pinkney....................	9 27	...	2 26	4 30	...	7 14
15½	Byfield	9 38	...	2 36	4 39	...	7 26
22	Fenny Compton....................	9 51	...	2 48	...	...	7 39
28½	Kineton	10 6	...	3 2	...	...	7 51
32½	Ettington	10 15	...	3 11	...	...	7 59
38	**STRATFORD-ON-AVON** arr.	10 26	...	3 22	...	...	8 8

A—Arrives 9.4 a.m. **B**—Arrives 4.10 p.m. **C**—Arrives 2.40 p.m. on Saturdays commencing June 24th. **SX**—Saturdays excepted. **SO**—Saturdays only.

Timetables from the period of the author's journey from Rushden to Kineton. *Author's collection*

KETTERING TO HUNTINGDON

This branch was first proposed in 1846 as part of the South Midland scheme. By that time George Hudson was in control of the MR and gave his support to the proposal, since he could see the threat posed by the Great Northern Railway's (GNR) line from London to York and its desire to expand westwards into traditional MR territory.

Parliament, of course, had the last word on what was to be built and by whom, and its decision was to allow the MR to build its Leicester to Hitchin line, providing it dropped its support for the South Midland scheme, which of course included the Kettering to Huntingdon line.

In 1862 Parliamentary powers were again sought by a new company, the Kettering & Thrapstone (sic) Railway, and were granted. A year later it changed its name to the Kettering, Thrapstone & Huntingdon Railway (KT&HR) and again received its Act. From the outset the line was to be worked by the MR under an agreement of 1866; it was also in that year that the 'e' from Thrapstone was dropped. (The KT&HR was eventually absorbed into the MR in 1897.) The long-term aim of the branch was to provide a service between Kettering and Cambridge, so running powers were obtained from the Great Eastern Railway (GER) to continue onwards from Huntingdon to Cambridge via St Ives; in fact, in the latter days of its life it became known as 'The Varsity Line'.

One other important factor in the promotion of this branch, in addition to provide a link to Huntingdon and Cambridge and keep the GNR at bay, was the discovery of large quantities of good-quality iron ore in the area between Kettering and Thrapston, which, coupled with the iron- and steel-making plants springing up in the area, meant new business for the MR.

The branch was built as a single line with passing loops at Butlin's Sidings (between Kettering and Cranford), Thrapston and Kimbolton. Stations were built at Cranford, Twywell, Thrapston, Raunds, Kimbolton, Long Stow, Grafham, Buckden and Huntingdon, only the first four being in Northamptonshire.

The line opened for goods traffic in February 1866 and for passenger services a month later. Because of the rural nature of the route, the passenger services provided can only be described as minimal, four or five trains a day being the order for most of its life. Raunds station, for example, was well over 1½ miles from the centre of the town. There were plans to extend the Higham Ferrers line and to make a junction with the KT&HR near Raunds station, and in so doing provide a new station near the town centre, but this came to nothing.

The timetable for 1921 shows some interesting footnotes: for example, one says that the train will only stop at Twywell and Cranford on Fridays and Bank Holidays! There was also at this time a once-a-day Kettering to Thrapston return service. At holiday times the branch did see through

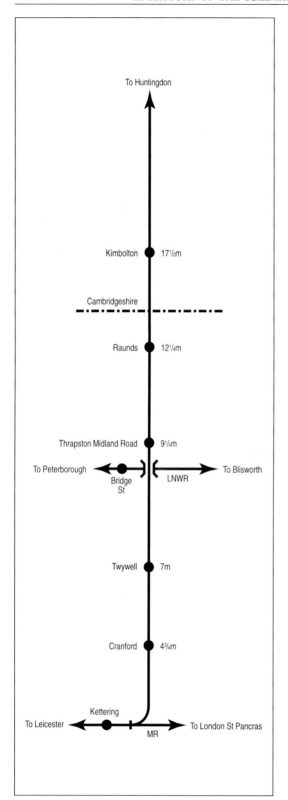

To Huntingdon

Kimbolton ● 17½m

Cambridgeshire

Raunds ● 12¼m

Thrapston Midland Road ● 9¼m

To Peterborough ← ●)(→ To Blisworth
Bridge LNWR
St

Twywell ● 7m

Cranford ● 4¾m

Kettering
To Leicester ← ● → To London St Pancras
MR

Kettering to Huntingdon (MR), opened February 1866 (distances from Kettering).

trains from the Midlands to Clacton-on-Sea, but these were very much the exception to the rule. In the 1930s these specials attracted the attention of a Mr J. Kite, and one of his photographs was published in the May 1957 edition of *Trains Illustrated*, showing a train at speed near Buckden double-headed by Midland 2-4-0s. Mr Kite submitted his photograph to the *LMS Magazine*, who pointed out that they couldn't publish it because it was against the rules to run these locomotives in tandem! Mr Kite concluded by saying that on future visits he found the train being hauled by 0-6-0s or double-headed with a 2-4-0 and an 0-6-0.

Although, as already mentioned, the passenger services were sparse, there was always a healthy goods traffic throughout the branch, together with the extra iron-ore workings from the western end of the line. In 1885 exchange sidings were built at Thrapston, where the line crossed the LNWR Peterborough line, exclusively for the exchange of iron-ore traffic.

The Second World War brought extra traffic to the line, not only with special troop trains but also for the transport of bombs and ammunition to an airfield between Kimbolton and Stow Longa; additional sidings were laid in at those two places to deal with this extra traffic. After the war life on the branch resumed its quiet existence, but not for long. The nationalisation of the country's railways led to a questioning of the viability of many lines and branches; as noted elsewhere, after the war road traffic began to rise steeply and the convenience of a car for someone living in the countryside weighed heavily against an infrequent service from remote stations.

The first closure, for both passenger and goods, came in July 1951 at Twywell, followed by Cranford for passengers in April 1956. The other two stations in the county, Thrapston

Right An early photograph of
Cranford station. *Author's collection*

Above An undated photograph of
Thrapston Midland Road: note the
depression in the platform face to
allow access to the crossing and the
other platform. *Les Hanson*

Left The signal box at Thrapston in
July 1958. The box remained in situ
for a number of years after the line
closed and was still there, in
reasonable condition, in the mid-
1980s. *R. M. Casserley*

Two views of Raunds station taken in July 1958. Passengers to and from the town with no transport were faced with a walk of more than a mile. *R. M. Casserley*

Northampton, Kettering, Thrapston, Huntingdon, ad Cambridge.—MIDLAND.

	WEEK DAYS ONLY.							WEEK DAYS ONLY.							
Leave		a m	a m	p m	p m		Leave			a m	p m	p m	p m		
NORTHAMPTON		7 25	9 40	12 25	4 50		Cambridge	Only stops		8 0	11 35	2 25	5 10		
Kettering		8 25	11 0	2 55	7 10		Histon	when required		8 10	—	2 35	5 2		
Cranford		8 37	11 12	b	7 22		Oakington	to take up		8 14	—	2 40	5 25		
Twywell		8 45	11 19	b	7 29		Long Stanton	passengers		8 20	—	2 46	5 31		
Thrapston		8 53	11 26	3 15	7 39		Swavesey	booked to		8 26	—	2 52	5 37		
Raunds		9 3	11 34	3 24	7 49		St. Ives	stations west		8 36	12 4	3 0	5 45		
Kimbolton		9 17	11 47	3 37	8 1		Huntingdon	of Huntingdon.		8 48	12 15	3 10	5 55		
Graffham		9 27	11 57	—	8 11		Buckden			8 56	c	3 18	6 3		
Buckden		9 34	12 4	—	8 17		Graffham			9 3	12 27	3 25	6 10		
Huntingdon	Only stops	9 46	12 15	3 55	8 27		Kimbolton			9 15	12 38	2 36	6 22		
St. Ives	when required	9 56	12 25	4 6	8 37		Raunds			9 26	c	3 47	6 32		
Swavesey	to set down	10 4	12 34	—	8 44		Thrapston			9 35	12 56	3 56	6 41		
Long Stanton	booked from	10 10	12 40	—	8 49		Twywell			9 42	c	4 3	6 43		
Oakington	stations west	10 15	12 47	—	8 54		Cranford			9 48	—	4 10	6 55		
Histon	of Huntingdon.	10 20	12 52	—	8 59		Ketterin			10 15	2 34	5 48	9 4		
Cambridge		10 30	1 2	4 35	9 10		NORTHAMPTON			11 40	3 15	6 35	9		

b Stops on Fridays and Saturdays, and when required to set down from beond Kettering. *c* Stops at Buckden and Raunds when required, and at Twywell to take up or beyond Kettering.

An 1873 timetable for the branch. *Author's collection*

and Raunds, closed for passenger traffic in June 1959, but managed to hang on to their goods facilities until the latter end of 1963.

The last commercial traffic was iron concentrate, which had previously been loaded at Higham Ferrers until November 1969, when it was transferred to Twywell.

The last train, in the official records, ran on 20 January 1978, but on 18 March of that year BR allowed a brake-van special to run from Wellingborough to Twywell, reversing at Kettering. The reason I know this is because I was invited to join this special for the price of £3.25. It was a bitterly cold day and the seven brake-vans all had their stoves lit to keep the passengers warm, though most spent the trip on the vans' verandas.

The unofficial 'Twywell Flyer' at Twywell in March 1978. *Author*

The New Viaduct, Thrapston

A postcard view of the new viaduct at Thrapston, which survives today. The LNWR's Peterborough line can just be seen crossing left to right in the middle distance.
Author's collection

Despite reassurances from local politicians that the track would be left in situ, within a year it was being lifted. Today much of the trackbed has disappeared under the plough, while west of Thrapston it was built on by the new A14. However, one of the major works on the line, the nine-arch brick viaduct crossing the River Nene at Thrapston, built in 1920 to replace the original wooden structure, still stands as a visible reminder of the line's history, as do the stations at Cranford, Thrapston and Kimbolton.

KETTERING TO MANTON

As we have seen in earlier chapters, the major railway companies were ever vigilant lest one of their rivals invade 'their' territory. The Midland Railway (MR) had the London & North Western Railway (LNWR) on its western flank, but on its eastern side was, increasingly, the Great Northern Railway (GNR), which was keen to move in and get its share of the coal traffic.

The early 1870s was a time of great railway expansion: between 1872 and 1874 the MR obtained Acts that allowed it to build two new lines. The first started from Nottingham and ran in an easterly direction before turning southwards and making a junction with its Syston–Peterborough line just west of Melton Mowbray. The second line started at Manton, also on the Syston–Peterborough line, and finished at a junction with its main line at Glendon, just north of Kettering.

There were various reasons for building these lines, some of which have been mentioned before; mainly it was an attempt to keep the GNR at bay and ensure that the MR would be able to carry the good-quality iron ore being quarried en route. They would also give the MR an alternative route for its London traffic; the main line between Wigston and Glendon was only double track (and still is) and this new line would avoid the Leicester area.

The line between Manton and Glendon is only 15¾ miles in length, but it was not an easy one to build from a civil engineering point of view. There were four tunnels, at

Wing (353 yards), Glaston (1m 82yd), Seaton (206 yards) and Corby (1m 180yd). With these tunnels came the associated cuttings, culverts, etc. The major work, started in March 1876, was the construction of the Welland Viaduct, now invariably referred to as Harringworth Viaduct. With a length of 1,275 yards (about three-quarters of a mile) it consists of 82 arches each of 40-foot span and with an average height of 57 feet. It is estimated that some 20 million bricks were used in its construction, all made on the spot from clay dug in the immediate vicinity of the viaduct.

When the work started the Bishop of Peterborough, the Rev William Magee, became concerned about the spiritual welfare of the thousands of navvies who had moved into the area. Consequently he set up what became known as the 'Bishop of Peterborough's Railway Mission'. He appointed a young curate to oversee this work, and for the years that the work was being done the Rev D. W. Barrett ministered to the men and their families. In 1879, with the work completed, he published his *Life and Work Amongst the Navvies*. Future historians owe a debt of gratitude to Rev Barrett because his book is a first-hand account of the working conditions that the navvies and their families had to endure. The book has long been out of print and copies are scarce; fortunately, in 2003, to celebrate the 125th anniversary of the viaduct, a facsimile copy was published by Silver Link.

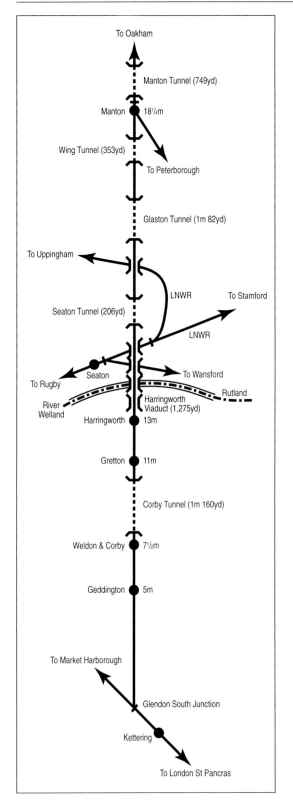

To Oakham

Manton Tunnel (749yd)

Manton ● 18¼m

Wing Tunnel (353yd)

To Peterborough

Glaston Tunnel (1m 82yd)

To Uppingham

LNWR   To Stamford

Seaton Tunnel (206yd)

LNWR

To Rugby   Seaton   To Wansford

River   Rutland
Welland
                Harringworth
Harringworth ● 13m   Viaduct (1,275yd)

Gretton ● 11m

Corby Tunnel (1m 160yd)

Weldon & Corby ● 7½m

Geddington ● 5m

To Market Harborough

Glendon South Junction

Kettering ●

To London St Pancras

Kettering to Manton (MR), opened in December 1879 (distances from Kettering).

Work started on the line in mid-1875, and despite setbacks caused by severe weather on several occasions, the work was completed on time. December 1879 saw the line opened for goods traffic, with up to 20 trains a day, in both directions. March 1880 saw the introduction of a local service between Kettering and Manton, then three months later, on 1 June, a completely new service was started between London, Kettering, Nottingham, Sheffield and Leeds. In time there evolved a separate service between Kettering and Nottingham.

Stations were opened at Harringworth, Gretton, Corby and Geddington, all on 1 March 1880. The passenger service provided was never great. In 1922, the last year in the life of the MR, passengers often had to change at Melton Mowbray or Manton. The late 1930s saw the best service for the stations on the line.

Corby, or to give it its correct name at the time of opening, Corby & Cottingham (it was to go through four more changes of name before becoming just plain Corby in March 1957), was just like the other villages on the line, but this was to change in a very dramatic way in the mid-1930s when it was decided to build one of the largest steel-making plants in the country there. The principal reason for selecting Corby was because of the large reserves of iron ore in the immediate area. Stewart & Lloyds, a Scottish company, was to become one of the country's leading producers of steel tubing and cold rolled strip, for which there was an ever-increasing demand, especially during the war years.

As when the line was being built, many more workers were needed, so history was to repeat itself with the construction and operation of the steelworks. Stewart & Lloyds looked to Scotland for these workers, and they came south in their hundreds together

Above Manton Junction in September 1982. The lines curving off to the left go to Peterborough, while those to the right go via Corby to Glendon South Junction on the Midland main line. *Author*

Below Manton station building in April 1999. *Author*

Above Glendon South Junction in July 1973, with the lines from Manton approaching round the curve. The lines in the centre are from Glendon North Junction signal box and joined the Manton line at Glendon South Junction signal box. *Author*

Below Harringworth Viaduct, 1,275 yards long and comprising 82 arches, photographed in September 1998. *Author*

Above Harringworth signal box and station photographed on a wet day from the top of the up home signal. *Author*

Above right and right Gretton's stone-built station from track level in July 1974, and the road side in September 1998. *Both author*

SPECIAL FARES

CORBY WORKS

British Rail and Corby District Council are delighted to announce the

Reopening of the

RAIL LINK

KETTERING

CORBY

FROM APRIL 13TH 1987
WITH CONNECTIONS TO
LONDON & LEICESTER

Fares
Corby-Kettering
50p single £1.00 return.
Children half price.
Pay on the train.
No discounts for
Railcards.
All fares and
facilities are subject
to alteration without
notice.

Examples of other fares
Corby-London £11.00 return.
Low saver not valid on Fridays
or on 07.13 (07.10 from 11.5.87)
Monday to Thursday
Corby-Leicester £3.40 return.
Not valid before 9.00am
Monday to Friday

Network SouthEast

British Rail

From
KETTERING ✱   OUT
To
CORBY ✱   ⇌
Route

Class
2ND   Adults
Ticket Type   ONE
CHEAPDY RTN CD NIL   Children
    Price   Date
    £1.00M 13. APR. 87
         1512 5272 M 06.54
Number
  4707   1857184700000
Valid
AS ADVERTISED
Tear ticket along perforation

British Rail

From
CORBY ✱   RTN
To.
KETTERING ✱   ⇌
Route

Class
2ND   Adults
Ticket Type   ONE
CHEAPDY RTN CD NIL   Children
    Price   Date
    £1.00M 13. APR. 87
         1512 5272 M 06.54
Number
  4707   1847185700000
Valid
AS ADVERTISED
Tear ticket along perforation

Left **Two Class 37 diesel locomotives leave Corby steelworks in July 1988, photographed from Corby North signal box.** *Author*

Below left **A handbill advertising the new service linking Kettering and Corby, and a ticket issued on the first day of the service.** *Both author's collection*

with their families. Before their arrival, Corby's population was just over a 1,000; in 2005 it was 56,000, explaining why much of Scottish culture and traditions are still very evident in the area.

Like all the rural rail services in the county, closure threatened, and the first two stations to close to passengers were Harringworth and Geddington, in November 1948. Gretton and, amazingly, Corby closed in April 1966. This left Corby with the distinction of being the only Parliamentary Constituency with no passenger rail service! After years of campaigning, BR (Network SouthEast) agreed to provide a shuttle service between Corby and Kettering, albeit with a financial subsidy from Corby Council. The service started on 13 April 1987 with an hourly service, and, with only a journey time of only 13 minutes, soon proved popular; ironically, its popularity was one of the factors that brought about the demise of the service, as the conductor just did not have the time to collect the fares, with the result that for many it was a free service. With losses mounting and the Council unwilling

to continue funding, the last train ran on 2 June 1990.

At the time the service started, the steelworks, facing increasing competition from abroad, was forced to make thousands redundant. This resulted in a dramatic downturn in rail traffic and the possibility of the line closing. However, with the modernisation of the signalling system on the main line in the 1980s, and closure of the line at weekends, the route came into its own again, as foreseen by the MR a century years earlier. In the late 1980s Railtrack, in its wisdom, singled the line between Kettering and Corby, thus hampering the line's capacity.

First started by InterCity and continued by Midland Mainline, a dedicated shuttle bus service now provides a direct link between Kettering station and Corby town centre.

Today the line is used as a diversionary route, and carries the small amount of steel traffic into and out of the remaining works at Corby and steam specials running over Harringworth Viaduct. Ironically, one of the increases in traffic in recent years has been trainloads of new cars from the continent, which are stored in Corby on acres of land where the old steelworks had been.

At the present time there seems little likelihood of Corby station re-opening for regular passenger services unless a new east-west service is introduced, in which case there is a possibility.

LODDINGTON BRANCH

Although it was intended to make only passing references to the ironstone quarrying in the county, this branch must be included.

Almost without exception, quarried ironstone was carried to the nearest railway line by the quarry company's own rail network, usually a narrow gauge system. The difference with the Loddington branch was that the Midland Railway (MR) built it as a standard gauge line specifically to serve the quarries, and it was never intended to provide a passenger service.

By 1873 quarrying was under way in the Cransley area, and in 1875 an ironworks was built and was in production two years later. Also in 1877, the MR, having obtained powers to construct the branch, built and opened what was to become the first section of the line, single track and just over a mile in length. It curved sharply away towards the west immediately south of Kettering station, then continued for a short distance past the ironworks at Cransley to a tipping dock. Here ironstone not intended for the ironworks could be loaded for other destinations.

The quality of the ironstone in the Cransley area was never of the best, and as a result new areas of ironstone, of higher quality, were being worked in the Loddington area, some 3 miles beyond Cransley. Initially the ironstone from these workings was brought to Cransley by a narrow gauge tramway.

In January 1893 the MR extended its

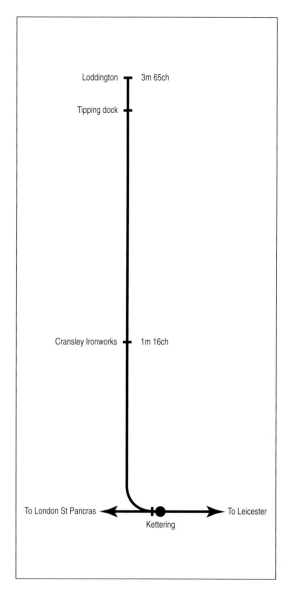

Loddington branch (MR), opened in February 1877 (distances from junction).

Standard gauge Hawthorn Leslie 0-6-0T No 3884 heads a load of iron ore at Loddington in April 1959 (above), which will be worked forward to Kettering by Ivatt Class 2 No 46495, a 15B loco. *Both H. C. Casserley*

CRANSLEY and LODDINGTON BRANCHES.

			MO a.m.		M a.m.		a.m.		QH p.m.		p.m.		QH p.m.		S p.m.	
KETTERING	..	dep.	7 30	..	8 30	..	11 20	..	..	..	2 35	..	..	..	5 40	..
Cransley	..	{ arr.	7 35	..	8 35	..	11 25	..	..	..	2 40	..	..	..	5 45	..
	..	{ dep.	8 20	..	9 5	..	11 50	..	12 45	..	3 0	..	3 55	..	6 10	..
LODDINGTON	..	arr.	8 30	..	9 15	..	12 0	..	12 55	..	3 10	..	4 5	..	6 20	..

			MO a.m.		M a.m.		QH p.m.		p.m.		QH p.m.		p.m.		S p.m.	
LODDINGTON	..	dep.	9 0	..	9 40	..	12 20	..	1 15	..	3 30	..	4 25	..	6 40	..
Cransley	..	{ arr.	9 10	..	9 50	..	12 30	..	..	..	3 40	..	4 35	..	..	..
	..	{ dep.	9 30	..	10 15	..	..	..	..	..	..	..	5 0	..	..	..
KETTERING	..	arr.	9 35	..	10 20	..	..	..	1 35	..	..	..	5 10	..	7 0	..

H—Bunker trips.

Above **A working timetable for the branch in 1914.**
Author's collection

Below George Cohen's scrapyard at Cransley in September 1974. D5909 is in the process of being cut up. *Author*

branch from Cransley to Loddington using, in part, the trackbed of the narrow gauge line. When the original section of the branch was opened the MR built a signal box at Cransley, but when the extension was opened it appears that the box closed and the line was operated as a single branch. The extension line did not make an end-on junction at the loading dock, but instead started between there and the ironworks. The end of the line was at Loddington, some 3 miles 65 chains from the junction with the main line at Kettering, the terminus being in the middle of an isolated field.

At the outset of the Second World War the quarrying company contemplated continuing its own rail system from Loddington to Pitsford, the idea being to transport all the ironstone from one point – Kettering – but this was never put into practice.

After the war, 'big is beautiful' thinking appeared and this spelled the end for small production units, which included ironworks. The works at Cransley ceased production at the end of November 1957, followed by their demolition. This could easily have been the end of the line, but the site of the old ironworks was taken over by George Cohen, Sons & Co, a name that was to take on a special significance to railway enthusiasts. George Cohen established a scrapyard there, which specialised in the scrapping of locomotives and rolling-stock. The demise of steam throughout the country meant that there were hundreds of locomotives with no further use, so the answer was to sell them for scrap; consequently locomotives from all over the country ended up at Cransley, and enthusiasts flocked to pay their last respects, which, if memory serves me right, was not welcomed by Cohen's!

It was on 18 May 1968 – a year that will always be associated with the demise of steam on BR – that the branch saw its first and only passenger train. A three-car DMU, full of railway enthusiasts, was allowed to travel up the entire length of the branch.

Much of the scrap metal from Cohen's was destined for the nearby steel plants at Corby, but when these closed in 1980 the scrap metal business lost its biggest market and decided to close. The section between Cransley and Loddington had closed in June 1970, and the original section from Kettering to Cransley followed in September 1980.

The history of the industrial locomotives that worked in the quarries has been well documented in the late Eric Tonks's books, but one locomotive that worked on the system perhaps warrants a particular mention. A metre gauge French locomotive, an 0-6-0T named *Cambrai*, had been bought in 1936 to work in the quarries. After their closure it went to other companies and, amazingly, escaped being scrapped. Today it can be seen, sadly not working, at the Narrow Gauge Railway Museum in Irchester Country Park.

As late as May 1998 it was still possible to walk the trackbed and find remains of this system between Cransley and Loddington. However, much of the first part of the branch has subsequently disappeared under new roads and housing estates.

HIGHAM FERRERS BRANCH

Northamptonshire's two principal industries were the production of iron and steel and the manufacture of boots and shoes. Almost every town and village in the county had some connection with the boot and shoe industry, Rushden and Higham Ferrers being no exception.

Rushden's population had risen dramatically from just under 4,000 in 1891 to some 13,000 by 1911. Much of the land at Higham Ferrers was owned by the Duchy of Lancaster, which is possibly why the growth of the shoe industry there was on a much smaller scale compared its neighbour.

With the output of the factories rising steeply, the problem of getting the finished goods away became a problem. The two nearest stations were at Irthlingborough on the LNWR's Peterborough branch and at Irchester on the MR main line, which had opened in 1857. Both stations were well over a mile from the town centres and both involved climbing hills, especially Irchester – no problem to today's modern transport, but a totally different situation for horses and carts.

The manufacturers approached the LNWR, but to no avail, and the MR was also not very interested. The MR had two problems at the time. First was the financial situation, which was not good, and second, from the operating point of view it did not want a branch starting almost at the bottom of what, for those days, was a steep climb to Sharnbrook Summit; trains coming on and off the branch would interrupt trains on the main line.

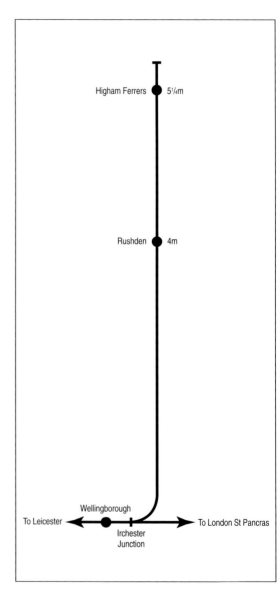

Higham Ferrers branch (MR), opened in September 1893 (distances from Wellingborough).

As we have already seen, the MR, like the LNWR, was suffering from congestion and had no alternative but to start quadrupling its lines through the county, and by December 1883 this had been done to the lines between Irchester and Wellingborough. The shoe manufacturers persisted with their requests, but still the MR held back. Eventually the railway company agreed to build a branch, but it was not until July 1890 that the necessary Act was passed by Parliament.

Strangely, the Act was called the Irchester to Raunds Branch and empowered the MR to build a double-track line from a junction north of Irchester to a junction on the Kettering–Huntingdon branch at Raunds. No mention of either Rushden or Higham Ferrers was made in the Act, and when the line was built it was single-track and got no further than Higham Ferrers. One gets the very strong impression that the MR was not really interested in building the line.

It was not until 1892 that building got under way. The branch opened for goods traffic officially on 1 September 1893, but in fact a short length near its junction with the main line had opened several months earlier in order to remove useful amounts of iron ore. Passenger services had to wait until 1 May the following year.

A limited amount of earthworks were undertaken beyond Higham Ferrers on the proposed extension to Raunds. In 2004 research brought to light a map showing the route of this extension, which proved that the MR did have serious intentions of continuing on to the Kettering–Huntingdon line.

The branch quickly settled down to a regular service of about 12 return trips, on weekdays only. Whatever doubts the MR had harboured about building the branch, there is no doubt that it turned in good profits over its life. Many of the raw materials for the boot and shoe industry, and the finished products, used the branch. Passenger numbers built up

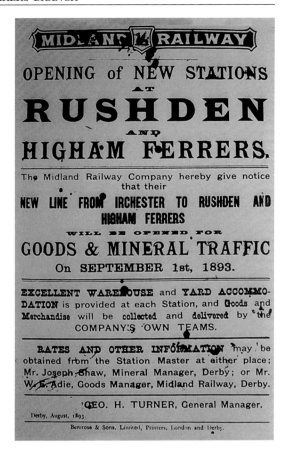

The opening notice for the branch. *Author's collection*

over the years, with the shoe industry providing another source of revenue for the railway. As early as 1934, one of Rushden's leading shoe manufacturers had chartered three special trains to take more than 1,000 employees and their families to Brighton for the day. These works specials continued after the war, but by then, as with the whole rail system, the increasing availability of cars for the man in the street began to take its toll on passenger numbers. For people travelling to Wellingborough it meant a long walk up to the town centre or a change of train if they were going to Northampton, and the car was so much more convenient

British Railways did make two attempts to increase patronage on the branch. The first came in the summer of 1952, when, on

Above Rushden station in April 1959. *R. M. Casserley*

Below Higham Ferrers station in June 1955. *R. M. Casserley*

Saturdays, it started a through service from Higham Ferrers to Leicester. This brought the sight of a large passenger locomotive with seven to nine coaches on the branch on a regular basis. Surprisingly, the through train did not work back to Higham; passengers had to return on the normal service trains and change at Wellingborough. Then in 1954 the usual pull-and-push loco with its two coaches was replaced by a three-coach DMU, but this did not stay very long and it was soon back to the old order, but not for very much longer.

In September 1958 BR announced the closure of the branch to passenger services, and the last regular trains ran on 13 June 1959. As the branch was my local railway I made sure that I was on the last train back to Wellingborough, then, if memory serves me correctly, I walked back to Rushden!

Surprisingly, once a year, holiday specials still used the line until 1964. The very last passenger train was an enthusiasts' special on 18 May 1968. Goods services continued until 1 November 1969, and even within a few days of closure trains were still arriving at Rushden with up to 20 wagonloads of assorted goods. The very last train on the branch was a trainload of iron concentrate from a special tipping dock that had been built at Higham Ferrers, which was carried to steelworks at Irlam and Etruria. The branch had opened with iron ore and closed with another iron raw material.

For the next 25 years nothing much happened, apart from the lifting of the track. The station and goods shed at Higham Ferrers were demolished and today there is no evidence that a railway ever existed there. However, at Rushden the station and goods shed remained, still the property of BR, until 1976, when both were acquired by the local Council.

At about the same time a group of local

A handbill dated October 1958. *Author's collection*

transport enthusiasts was formed, and in 1985 the Council agreed to this group renting the station. Since that time the Rushden Historical Transport Society has slowly renovated the building, laid track, acquired locomotives and rolling-stock and become a centre for real ales!

In 2005 a new road was built through what had been the goods yard at Rushden, thus separating the station and the goods shed, which is still owned by the Council.

For many years the Transport Society has had plans to extend the line towards Higham Ferrers and even to return to Wellingborough. Sadly, with more and more of the remaining trackbed being built on, there seems little possibility of this happening.

NORTHAMPTON TO BEDFORD

The early days of the railways in this country were often marked by the opposition of the landed gentry and local clergy. As time passed, the degree of opposition lessened as it became obvious that, not only were the railways here to stay, but also they could be profitable.

There had been talk about a line linking Bedford, Northampton and Leamington, and an approach was made to the LNWR in 1859, but this came to nothing. However, with the growth of railways throughout the country becoming increasingly apparent, another attempt was made to see what could be done about linking the two county towns.

On Friday 19 August 1864 a large meeting of landowners and other interested gentlemen gathered at what was described as 'an informal meeting' at the Bull Inn in Olney to consider this question. It is interesting to see how worldly wise this group had become, because the minutes include the phrase 'desirable that the line should be worked by the Midland Railway'.

There appears to have been only one objection to the proposed route. The Marquis of Northampton did not want the railway running across his land at Yardley, and demanded that it be diverted. This was acceptable to the proposers since it meant that the line could now run much closer to the centre of Olney.

The company duly applied to Parliament and the Bedford and Northampton Railway Act was passed in July 1865, whereupon there was much celebrating at Olney, with bands marching through the town and the church bells being rung at intervals from dawn to dusk!

There were to be three stations between Northampton and Bedford, at Horton (Piddington), Olney and Turvey. It is interesting to note that Horton was in Northamptonshire, Olney in Buckinghamshire, and Turvey in Bedfordshire.

To make a real impression on the inhabitants of Northampton, the Midland Railway (MR) built a new station in St John's Street in the grounds of St John's Hospital and linked it to the town centre by a new road called Guildhall Rd. The new station replaced the earlier, much smaller affair that had served the MR when it had opened its service from Wellingborough and Kettering in 1866. It was a rather grand affair described as 'having been built on fourteen arches and having a highly ornamental entrance portico, which embodies a curious mixture of rectangular and circular pillars'. The station was on a curve, and just beyond it the MR built a carriage shed, most of which, above ground level, was of wood. The Act included provision for extensions beyond the carriage shed, but these options were never taken up. One interesting feature of the station was that, underneath it, the MR built a bonded warehouse.

For its day the branch had quite severe gradients, but it was never intended to be a main line, just a rural link and to keep rivals at bay – in fact, it had been described as little more than a glorified contractor's line. It was some 20 miles in length, having its southern junction not at Bedford station, but at Oakley Junction, some 1½ miles north of Bedford.

With the works completed, it was announced that the line would open on 1 May 1872. This was followed by notices saying that the opening had been postponed 'until further notice'. However, on 10 June of that year the line opened with the usual celebrations, although it must be said that the station at Northampton had not been completed.

At the half-yearly meeting of the company held in September 1872, the Chairman said how liberal the MR had been in running five trains a day in each direction! Although that number did increase over the years – six in 1922 and seven by 1938 – the service could only be described as minimal.

With the Grouping in 1923, the MR became part of the LMS. For some years not much changed, but then the LMS decided to close St John's station and divert all its passenger services to Northampton Castle. Closure duly took place on 3 July 1939. One consequence was that the junction between the MR and the LNWR at Hardingstone had to be reversed in order to allow the MR trains from Bedford to reach Castle station.

During the war years the line was probably busier than it had ever been in its life, but surprisingly in August 1940 the LMS closed the down line between Turvey and Olney, using it as a siding. This meant that all traffic had to use the up line, that running towards Bedford. Possibly because of the rural nature of the line, valuable war materials could be safely stored in the siding.

Once the war was over, like so many rural lines in the county, the closure programme started. However, first an attempt was made to improve the finances of the line by the

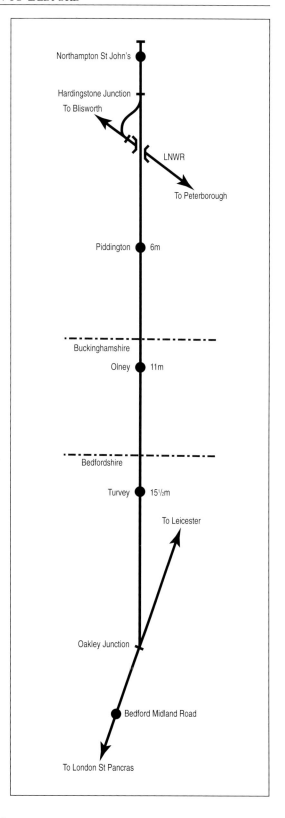

Northampton to Bedford (MR), opened in June 1872 (distances from Northampton).

Above St John's station in March 1939. The dray is probably at the bonded warehouse that was located beneath the station. *Bill Meredith*

Below St John's signal box and turntable in March 1939. *Bill Meredith*

Above right The MR locomotive shed beside the LNWR line in March 1939, with the line to St John's curving away to the right. The building is now a listed structure, though sadly it was damaged by fire in 2000. *Bill Meredith*

Below right The timetable of diesel trains for June–September 1960. *Author's collection*

introduction, in 1958, of diesel railcars, and an increase in the number of trains to nine. Additionally it was proposed to build a new halt at Newton Blossomville, and British Railways got as far as publishing handbills showing the location of the halt and local fares, but it all came to nothing.

St John's station was demolished at the end of 1960 and the site is now another car park. Had the demolition been delayed there is a chance that this splendid building might have been preserved.

Closure of the three intermediate stations for passenger services came on 5 March 1962.

BEDFORD AND NORTHAMPTON — Second Class only

WEEKDAYS ONLY

							SX	SX	SO	SO	SX	SO	SX			
		am		am	am	am	am	pm	pm	pm	pm	pm	pm	pm	pm
BEDFORD Midland Road ...dep.	6 40	...	8 10	9 49	11 26	11 30	12 40	1 17	1 40	3 20	4 50	6 53	8 35		
Turvey	6 50	...	8 24	9 59	11 36	11 40	12 50	1 27	1 52	3 30	5 0	7 03	8 45		
Olney	6 58	...	8 32	10 07	11 44	11 48	12 58	1 35	2 0	3 38	5 8	7 11	8 58		
Piddington	...	...	...	10 15	11 52	11 56	1 6	1 43	2 11	3 45	...	...	...		
NORTHAMPTON Bridge Street	7 13	...	8 48	10 24	12 1	12 05	1 15	1 52	2 21	3 55	5 23	7 26	9 08		
" Castle ... arr.	7 17	...	8 51	10 27	12 4	12 08	1 18	1 55	2 25	3 58	5 27	7 30	9 12		

		SO	SX	SX	SO	SX		SX	SO	SO	SX			FX	FO
	am	am	am	am	am	pm	pm	pm	pm	pm	pm	pm	pm	pm	pm
NORTHAMPTON Castle ...dep.	7 56	7 56	9 05	10 25	10 38	12 12	2 20	2 22	3 25	4 02	6 07	7 40	9 18	9 30	
" Bridge Street	7 58	7 58	9 07	10 27	10 40	12 14	2 22	2 24	3 27	4 04	6 09	7 42	9 20	9 32	
Piddington	...	...	9 16	10 36	10 49	12 23	2 33	2 33	3 36	...	...	...	...	...	
Olney	8 14	8 14	9 24	10 44	10 57	12 31	2 41	2 41	3 44	4 20	6 25	7 58	9 36	9 48	
Turvey	8 24	8 24	9 32	10 52	11 05	12 39	2 49	2 49	3 52	4 28	6 33	8 06	9 44	9 57	
BEDFORD Midland Road ...arr.	8 38	8 36	9 43	11 3	11 16	12 50	3 3	3 3	4 3	4 39	6 44	8 17	9 55	10 10	

FX—Fridays excepted   FO—Fridays only   SO—Saturdays only   SX—Saturdays excepted

BEDFORD AND HITCHIN — Second Class only

WEEKDAYS ONLY

							SO	SX	SO	SO	SX	SO	SX		SO	SX
		am	am	am	am	pm	pm	pm	pm	pm	pm			pm	pm
BEDFORD Midland Road ...dep.	6 20	8 45	10 35	10 43	12 20	12 22	2 19	2 23	4 23	4 30		5 58	6 02		
Cardington	6 25	8 50	10 40	10 48	12 25	12 27	2 24	2 28	4 28	4 35		6 03	6 07		
Southill	6 32	8 53	10 47	10 55	12 32	12 34	2 31	2 34	4 35	4 42		6 10	6 14		
Shefford	6 37	9 02	10 52	11 00	12 38	12 39	2 36	2 40	4 40	4 47		6 15	6 19		
Henlow Camp ...	6 42	9 07	10 57	11 05	12 42	12 44	2 41	2 45	4 45	4 52		6 20	6 24		
HITCHIN ... ...arr.	6 50	9 15	11 09	11 13	12 50	12 56	2 51	2 53	4 53	5 01		6 28	6 32		

		SX	SO	SO	SX	SX		SO		SO	SX	SO	SX
	am	am	am	am	am	pm		pm		pm	pm	pm	pm
HITCHIN ... ...dep.	7 35	9 30	9 30	11 40	11 45	1 20	...	1 35	3 45	5 20	5 25	7 00	7 05
Henlow Camp ...	7 42	9 37	9 37	11 47	11 52	1 27	...	1 42	3 52	5 28	5 32	7 07	7 12
Shefford	7 47	9 42	9 42	11 52	11 57	1 32	...	1 47	3 57	5 33	5 37	7 12	7 17
Southill	7 51	9 46	9 47	11 56	12 01	1 36	...	1 51	4 01	5 38	5 41	7 16	7 21
Cardington	7 58	9 53	9 54	12 03	12 08	1 43	...	1 58	4 08	5 45	5 48	7 23	7 28
BEDFORD Midland Road ...arr.	8 04	9 59	10 02	12 09	12 14	1 49	...	2 04	4 17	5 53	5 54	7 29	7 34

SO—Saturdays only   SX—Saturdays excepted

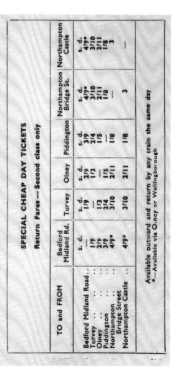

A undated winter scene at Piddington, with No 44691 heading a lightweight goods through the station towards Bedford. *F. G Cockman*

The exterior of Piddington station in October 1979. *Author*

There was a large Ministry of Defence (MoD) store at Piddington, and the traffic to this ensured that the part of the line between Northampton and Piddington remained open. In February 1968 this stretch of line was formally handed over to the MoD. Track-lifting on this section, other than a short section to Brackmills, was completed by 1986. In October 1979 the Army laid on a special trip for railway enthusiasts between the old Power Station at Northampton and Piddington, using an Army railbus, which gave me my last opportunity to travel over part of this branch.

At the other end of the line, between Piddington and Oakley Junction, closure came in January 1964. Piddington and Turvey stations have survived and are now in private hands, while part of the trackbed east of Turvey station is now used by the Stevington & Turvey Light Railway, a narrow gauge line. Nearer to Bedford the trackbed has become the Stevington Country Walk.

At the time of writing there is still one remaining structure of MR origin in Northampton, a small locomotive depot that was used in recent years as a BR welding school. In 1995 the building was given a Grade 2 listing, but in 2000 arsonists set fire to it; although much of the structure was saved, its future looks uncertain.

In recent years there has been talk of re-opening the line throughout, but I suspect it will come to nothing, despite the fact that a high proportion of the trackbed is still in situ.

Great Central Railway

The last main line to come through the county, and sadly the first to close, was the Great Central Railway (GCR). For the origins of this company we need to go back to January 1847, and the formation of the Manchester, Sheffield & Lincolnshire Railway (MSLR), which, as its name suggests, was basically just a cross-country line.

In 1853 Edward Watkin became its General Manager, but then took up a post overseas. However, he was back in the UK by 1863 and took up the same position. A year later he became the Chairman of the MSLR. Watkin was a man not unlike the legendary George Hudson, who, some 20 years earlier, had taken the railway world by storm. Watkin knew what he wanted to achieve and was not above some dubious ways of getting there. His two main ambitions seemed to be to put the MSLR in the big league by having its own line to London, and to get involved with proposals for a Channel Tunnel.

To achieve his first ambition he needed to be in a position where he could influence events. He therefore became Chairman of three railway companies, the South Eastern Railway in 1866, the Metropolitan Railway in 1872, and the East London Railway in 1878. One of his reasons for wanting his own line to London was that the MSLR had come to an arrangement in 1857 with the Great Northern Railway (GNR) to carry MSLR traffic to London. Like the MR, which had a similar arrangement with the GNR in earlier days, the MSLR's traffic did not get priority over that of the GNR.

It must be remembered that while Watkin was proposing his main line into London from the north, the LNWR, MR and GNR were already well established. Notwithstanding that fact, Watkin pressed on with his plans, and in later years the MSLR was to become known as the Money, Sunk and Lost Railway!

Watkin must have been quite a dynamic character, because despite all of his railway commitments he still found time to be a Liberal MP for three different constituencies between the years 1857-95. He was knighted in 1868 and was made a baronet in 1880.

The MSLR applied to Parliament for powers to build its proposed London Extension and failed in its first attempt. Its second attempt in March 1893 was successful. The Act authorised the building of the new line from Annesley (north of Nottingham) to a junction with the Metropolitan Railway (Met) at Quainton Road (north of Aylesbury). From this latter point the MSLR had running powers over the Met as far as Canfield Place (near Finchley Road), where it would have its own lines for the 2 miles to its own station at Marylebone. This last stretch presented the GCR with a problem, as the route lay through the famous Lord's Cricket Ground! In the past railways had swept all aside – little or nothing got in their way. But how could the GCR placate the furious members? The answer was to tunnel under the ground and to do it in the winter so as to keep disturbance to a minimum. As a further sop

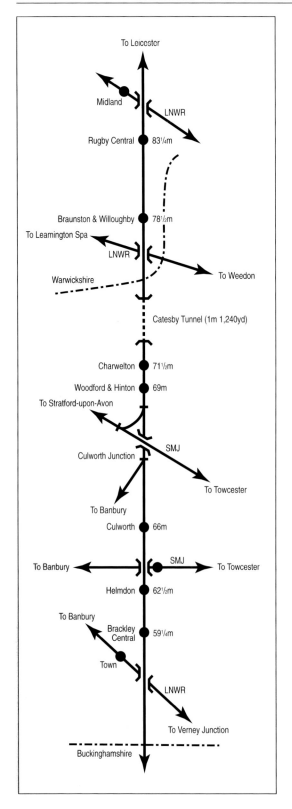

To Leicester

Midland

Rugby Central ● 83¼m

LNWR

Braunston & Willoughby ● 78½m

To Leamington Spa

LNWR

To Weedon

Warwickshire

Catesby Tunnel (1m 1,240yd)

Charwelton ● 71½m

Woodford & Hinton ● 69m

To Stratford-upon-Avon

SMJ

Culworth Junction

To Towcester

To Banbury

Culworth ● 66m

SMJ

To Banbury

To Towcester

Helmdon ● 62½m

To Banbury

Brackley Central ● 59¼m

Town

LNWR

To Verney Junction

Buckinghamshire

Great Central Railway, opened in July 1898 (distances from London Marylebone).

to the cricketers, the GCR bought an orphanage and its grounds, which stood next to Lord's, and presented it to the MCC. What happened to the children is not known!

The route was to run through the western side of Northamptonshire, with stations at Charwelton, Woodford & Hinton (later Woodford Halse), Culworth, Helmdon and Brackley. Although the length of line through the county was only 15 miles, it required several large engineering constructions. Starting in the north, there was the 3,000–yard tunnel at Catesby. The owner of Catesby House had stipulated how far the tunnel and its portals were to be from the house (the house was at one time owned by Robert Catesby, one of the main conspirators of the Gunpowder Plot). Moving south, there were water troughs at Charwelton, a nine-arch viaduct at Helmdon, and a 756-foot viaduct at Brackley, with 20 arches and two plate girder spans. Sadly, the viaduct at Brackley was demolished in the late 1970s, but the tunnel and the other viaduct at Helmdon are still extant.

Until the arrival of the railway, the village of Woodford had been just like many small villages in the western part of the county. The 1891 Census shows a population of 527, while ten years later it had risen to 1,220, this dramatic increase being directly due to the railway. Because Woodford was roughly midway between the Derbyshire/Nottinghamshire coalfields and London, it was chosen by the MSLR (renamed the Great Central Railway in 1897) as the site for a locomotive depot with facilities for up to 50 locomotives, a wagon repair workshop and extensive sidings. To accommodate all the extra workers and their families, upwards of 200 terraced houses were built in the village.

Work started on the Extension in

Above Helmdon station in June 1958, looking towards Brackley. *R. M. Casserley*

Below A telephoto shot of Brackley Viaduct in October 1977, shortly before its demolition. *Author*

Below Charwelton station looking south in July 1946, showing to good effect the typical GCR signal box and 'island' platform. *R. M. Casserley*

November 1894 and for the first time much of the construction work was helped by the introduction of mechanical earth-moving machinery; prior to this all earthworks had been done by manual labour. The plan for this new route was that it was to be as straight as possible and that gradients were to be kept to a maximum of 1 in 176, and this was certainly the case throughout the county.

On 25 July 1898 the line opened for coal traffic only; it is said that this was done in order that the heavier coal trains would help to settle and consolidate the trackbed. Passenger services had to wait until 15 March 1899, with up to 14 trains a day in each direction, though not every one stopped at all the stations. By now Watkin was in retirement, and while he lived to see his London Extension built and running, his dreams of running his trains through the Channel Tunnel came to naught. He died in 1901 at the age of 81.

At the same time as the opening of the line, a short curve from south of Woodford &

Hinton station turned westward and joined the East & West Junction Railway (E&WJR) near Byfield; this line had opened in 1873 from Towcester to Stratford-upon-Avon (and became part of the SMJ). At almost the same time another, west-to-south, curve opened, enabling trains to run direct from Marylebone to Stratford, but passenger services used this curve for only a few weeks in August 1899, and it was closed completely in October 1900.

Another branch left the main line south of Woodford at Culworth Junction, linking the GCR with Banbury on the GWR main line, a distance of just over 8 miles. This opened for through traffic in 1900, and in later years two small platforms/halts were added, at Chalcombe Road in April 1911 and Eydon Road in October 1913. Although this branch line was built by the GCR, it was paid for by the GWR.

The way was now open for long-distance, cross-country trains, but there were also local services from Woodford to Stratford and Banbury, so to keep these clear of the main line an extra platform was built at Woodford, connected by a footbridge. This was unusual, since the GCR had built its other stations on the 'island' pattern between the running lines,

Woodford Halse station in August 1961, with the additional platform on the extreme left. Thompson 'B1' No 61206 has arrived with a Nottingham-Marylebone train, and the engine crews are changing over. *F. G. Cockman*

which meant only one platform was needed and access to it was from either a road overbridge or underbridge.

In 1923, with the advent of the Grouping, the GCR became part of the London & North Eastern Railway (LNER), which meant that LNER locomotives and rolling-stock could be seen at both sides of the county.

It was noted in the chapter on the Kettering to Manton line how the church became concerned for the spiritual welfare of the navvies and their families. A similar situation arose with the building of the GCR line. This time not only were the Anglicans involved, but also the Moravians. This branch of the Christian Church had started in Eastern Bohemia and had a great influence on John and Charles Wesley, the founders of the Methodist Church. The Moravians settled in Woodford after their initial work with the navvies was over, and built their own church.

With the outbreak of the Second World War the former GCR route took on a new importance, since it traversed large stretches of rural England and as such was less likely to suffer from bombing. Such was the increase in freight traffic that larger marshalling yards were built at Woodford in 1941.

After the war, and with nationalisation of the railways in 1948, the same pattern of station and line closures occurred as we have seen elsewhere. With nationalisation the LNER became part of the Eastern Region of British Railways, and things carried on as before until 1958, when the GCR route was transferred to one of its former rivals, the LMS, now the London Midland Region of BR. Attempts were made to modernise some passenger services by the introduction of DMUs, but it was to no avail. The motor industry was taking all sorts of traffic from the railways and the inevitable closure programme started except, in this case, it was not just the stations that closed – the main line was to go

A BR poster from June 1962. *Author's collection*

as well. The last main line to arrive in London was to be the first to close.

However, the late 1950s and early 1960s saw a boom on the freight side. As early as 1947 BR had introduced fast regular freight services between Annesley and Woodford. With the introduction of the Class '9F' steam locomotives, these freight trains could, and did, run to quite fast timings such that they became known as the 'Runners' or 'Windcutters'. In some cases the crews could manage two return trips every day.

With BR introducing diesel locomotion, a half-hearted attempt was made to modernise Woodford depot to deal with them, but it did not get very far and the most that Woodford saw of diesel traction was to be four small shunting engines. The yards and locomotive depot closed in 1965.

Above Brackley station looking north in June 1958 with its familiar row of pines, which survive today, as do the station buildings. *R. M. Casserley*

Below Thompson 'B1' No 61106 waits at Brackley with a Nottingham train in July 1961. *F. G. Cockman*

By now the writing was on the wall and final closure became inevitable. The two halts on the Banbury branch had closed in 1956, while the first closure on the main line was Culworth in 1958. Next came Charwelton and Helmdon, both in March 1963. The two principal stations, Woodford and Brackley, survived until September 1966, the last trains at Woodford running on 4 September of that year.

With the closure of the line and its stations south of Rugby complete, BR continued to run a service of DMUs between Rugby and Nottingham, but these only lasted for a few more years, and that section of the old GCR closed in May 1969.

In conclusion it is worth recalling an aspect of rail business that was somewhat unusual but was popular in the county. The GCR was noted for its ability to spot new potentials for business and to make sure it was well advertised. The area of Northamptonshire through which the line ran was hunting country, and several well-known hunts, including the Bicester and the Grafton, bordered the railway, mainly to the west and east. The GCR went so far as to issue special timetables setting out arrangements for hunts and laying on special trains for the riders and their horses. The days when one could live in London and have a day's hunting in the country had arrived!

Although it is well outside the county, one can still ride part of the old GCR between Leicester and Loughborough thanks to the preserved 'Great Central Railway'. One further link with the early days of the GCR came to light in 2005. While driving through the tiny village of Halse – north of Brackley – I noticed a 'tin tabernacle'. Subsequent research (for which I am indebted to Mrs Hudson of Brackley History Society) revealed the fact that this had been built as a community centre for the navvies working on the London Extension. When the work was finished, a railway enthusiast, the Earl of Ellesmere, bought the hall and presented it to the villagers for use as a church. Today 'Halse Cathedral', as it is called by the locals, is still used for church services and as a community centre.

For several years there has been talk of re-opening parts of the old GCR as a freight route that would relieve the West Coast Main Line, but I suspect that this will come to nothing.

The 'tin tabernacle' at Halse, known locally as 'Halse Cathedral', photographed in August 2005. *Author*

GREAT WESTERN RAILWAY

The year 1845 saw the start of what was to become known as 'The Railway Mania'. Until 1844 Parliament had allowed railways to develop almost unhindered and it was becoming obvious that things were getting out of hand. The Prime Minister, Mr Gladstone, in introducing an Act that suggested the purchase of the railways by the state – in effect nationalisation – appears to have brought some common sense to the whole scene, although it did not deter the promoters of new lines, because in 1845 more than 2,800 miles of new railways were authorised by Parliament, virtually doubling what had already been built. During this period there was a clash between two of the big players, namely the London & Birmingham Railway (L&B) and the Great Western Railway (GWR). The former, being first on the scene, had the monopoly of the traffic between the two cities. However, the GWR was expanding its empire and was looking to see how it could move in on Birmingham, which, it must be remembered, was Britain's second city.

A concern for the L&B was the fact that the GWR was a broad gauge railway and wanted this gauge to be used throughout the railway world. After some dithering by Parliament, the Government set up a three-man Commission to decide which gauge should become the standard. Broad gauge was 7ft 0¼in, compared with what was initially called the narrow gauge of 4ft 8½in. At the time that the Committee was deliberating,

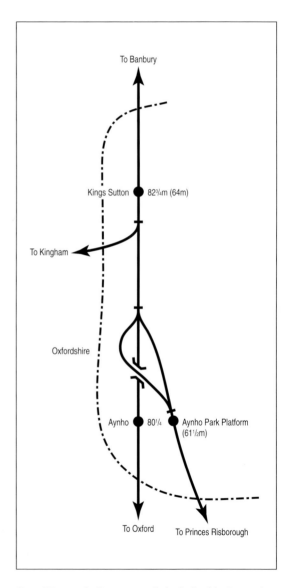

Great Western Railway, opened via Oxford in September 1850 (distances from London Paddington via Oxford and, in brackets, via Princes Risborough).

there were only 274 miles of broad gauge line in use against 1,901 miles of narrow gauge. After some trials the Commission reported, in 1846, that while there was much to be said for the broad gauge, on balance it had decided to recommend that the narrow gauge become the standard. This decision was to effect the few miles of the GWR that ran through the western tip of Northamptonshire.

That line was, to be precise, the Oxford & Rugby Railway (O&R), which obtained its Act in August 1845, but became part of the GWR a year later. This line never got further north than Fenny Compton, which was where another company, the Birmingham & Oxford Junction (B&OJ) intended to link up with the O&R; the B&OJ also became part of the GWR in 1846.

The first part of the new route, between Oxford and Banbury, opened in September 1850. Despite the decision of the Gauge Commission, the GWR built the line as single-track in broad gauge! At the outset there were only three stations between Oxford and Banbury, at Woodstock Road, Heyford and Aynho, and of these only Aynho was in Northamptonshire. As time passed the GWR had to accept the fact that its broad gauge was doomed, and began to convert its lines to standard gauge. By 1852 the line between Oxford and Banbury had been converted to mixed gauge, then in 1856 it was doubled, and in April 1869 the broad gauge was abandoned.

Interestingly, Kings Sutton station did not open until 1 June 1872. Obviously the GWR had not considered that the village warranted a station when the line was opened, or indeed when the Banbury & Cheltenham Direct line opened between Chipping Norton and Kings Sutton in April 1887. It is still something of a mystery why the station was built, since it was, and still is, in a very rural part of the county, with Banbury only a few miles away. There was a considerable amount of iron-ore quarrying in the area, but that alone would not have justified a station.

The GWR was often referred to as the 'Great Way Round', and this was true of its services between London and Birmingham, which ran via Didcot and Oxford. As we saw in the previous chapter, the GWR enjoyed a happy working relationship with the GCR, and this was further cemented when a GWR/GCR Joint Committee was formed in 1899. This led to the construction of a new joint line from Northolt, in west London, to Princes Risborough, from where GWR trains could use their own line to Oxford, thereby avoiding the original route via Didcot and shortening the distance to Birmingham by 8 miles. The Joint line then continued

An early undated photograph of Kings Sutton station.
Author's collection

Above **Aynho station in April 1981 with the Princes Risborough line flyover in the background. At the time the station was being used by a coal merchant, but has subsequently become a private residence.** *Author*

Left **The last remaining structure at Aynho Park Halt is the old booking office on the up side, photographed in October 2001.** *Author*

northwards from Princes Risborough to Ashendon, where there was a link to the GCR main line and from where, in 1910, the GWR constructed its own line onward to the original 1850 line at Aynho. There a 50-yard single-span bridge carried the down line over the 1850 lines to reach the down main line to Banbury. With the opening of this new line the distance saved was in the order of 20 miles, making the GWR route to Birmingham 2 miles shorter than the L&B/LNWR route from Euston. At last the

GWR could compete with the LNWR, and continued to do so until the electrification of the Euston route in the 1960s.

With the opening of the Ashendon to Aynho line came several new stations. There was just one in Northamptonshire, at Aynho, which was called Aynho Park Platform to avoid confusion with its near neighbour on the main line. The opening of the new line meant that passengers from Kings Sutton and Aynho now had a choice of route to London.

The Grouping and nationalisation came and went with only small changes to the services. Then the start of the closure programme began to make its presence felt. First to go was the passenger service between Kings Sutton and Chipping Norton, withdrawn in 1951. Then came the closure of Aynho Park Platform in January 1963, followed by Aynho in November 1964. At the present time the station at Aynho still stands, as does, amazingly, the booking office at Aynho Park Platform, together with some of the original iron railings.

It was said earlier that the reason why the GWR built a station at Kings Sutton was a mystery. An even greater mystery is the fact that it is still open today, one of the five within the county to survive. In 1963 the station buildings were demolished, together with the footbridge, although when visited recently a waiting shelter on the down side still stands. Today's passengers now have to cross the lines at track level. One suspects that BR never expected the station, which had become an unstaffed halt, to survive.

A further rationalisation of the route in 1968 saw the line between Bicester and Aynho being singled. With rail privatisation the route become part of Chiltern Railways (CR). This company saw the potential, as the GWR had in earlier years, for increasing its share of traffic between London and Birmingham, but one of the problems that CR inherited was the single-line section, which restricted traffic flows. In 2002 permission was granted to enable this 9-mile section to be doubled. Once completed, CR has been able to increase the frequency of its services, while the upgrading of the WCML in recent years, with its attendant delays, has enabled CR to capture a larger share of the passenger traffic.

Today Kings Sutton enjoys a limited service to Paddington, while the majority of train reach the capital at Marylebone. Whatever one's views are on the question of privatisation, it is highly unlikely that the improvement to the services on this route would have happened in BR days. Finally, Kings Sutton saw a new footbridge erected at the beginning of June 2006.

Kings Sutton station in June 2006, with its replacement footbridge, looking south. *Author*

STAMFORD & ESSENDINE RAILWAY

One could be forgiven for asking what this railway has to do with Northamptonshire, but, as we shall see, an extension of this small railway did come into the county at its eastern end.

First let us go back to the days when Stamford was an important staging post on the Great North Road (today's A1). As such, people assumed that when the railways came northwards Stamford would again play an important role.

The first railway at Stamford was the Midland Railway's (MR) cross-country line from Syston to Peterborough in 1846; at first this was only an isolated section between Stamford and Peterborough because Lord Harborough objected to the MR's route, so the company had to build a deviation at Saxby in order to appease His Lordship, which resulted in through services having to wait until 1848.

At this period various schemes were planned to provide a direct connection between the capital and York. At that time the only way was via the London & North Western Railway (LNWR) from Euston to Rugby, then by the MR to Normanton, and finally the York & North Midland Railway. The latter two companies were under the control of George Hudson, and he was not prepared to give up his monopoly without a struggle, but despite some of his infamous 'wheeling and dealing' he lost. What was to become the Great Northern Railway (GNR) received its Act of Parliament in June 1846,

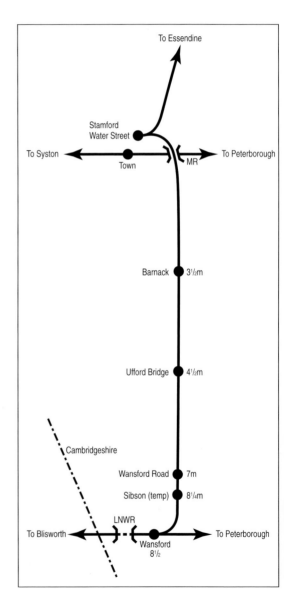

Stamford & Essendine Railway (Sibson branch) opened in August 1867 (distances from Stamford).

Above The grandiose station at Stamford East in June 2005, now in use as a private residence. *Author*

Below Ivatt Class 'C12' 4-4-2 No 67376 at Stamford East on the last day of services to Essendine. *F. G. Cockman*

and opened between London and Retford in August 1852. The route bypassed Stamford and went instead through Peterborough. The reason was claimed to be that the Marquis of Exeter did not want the railway on part of his estate; perhaps fresh in the memories of the townsfolk were the abovementioned problems with Lord Harborough. In 1966, however, the then Marquis, in a letter to *The Railway Magazine*, attempted to put the record straight by saying that the reason was purely to do with engineering. However, subsequent writing on the subject still leaves some doubts.

Stamford still wanted connections to the main line, and in August 1853 the Stamford & Essendine Railway (S&ER) obtained its Act of Parliament authorising the construction of a line just over 3 miles in length between

Barnack station in June 1999, now a private residence.
Author

Stamford, where it had its own station, and Essendine, on the GNR main line, with two intermediate stations. Work eventually started in 1855, and the line opened in November 1856, with the GNR working the line from the outset.

The station at Stamford was a grand affair, in keeping with the town's character and possibly due to the fact that the Marquis was a major shareholder in the company! It appears that for many years engines were not allowed to enter the train shed: the practice was for incoming trains to be stopped outside at a ticket platform and have their engines uncoupled. The carriages were then allowed to run into the station by gravity after the locomotive, which had run round its train, gave them a little nudge. The guard stopped the train at the platform by using his brake. All this came to a sudden end (literally) in 1896 when something went wrong and the carriages crashed into and through the buffer

stops! The compensation bill must have made a big hole in that year's revenue.

It was anticipated that the majority of passenger traffic would be between Stamford and London, yet building a line to Essendine not only meant that passengers had further to travel, but the junction at Essendine faced northward, so no through running was possible! The S&ER therefore sought to partially overcome the first point by proposing a new line southwards from Stamford, which would make a junction with the LNWR's Blisworth to Peterborough line at Wansford. Powers for this branch were granted in July 1864.

Although laid for double track, it was single-track throughout its life. At just over 8 miles in length, the Sibson branch, as it was referred to, had intermediate stations at Barnack, Ufford Bridge and Wansford Road. The approach to Wansford was from the east, which again meant that no through running was possible without reversing. Opening took place in August 1867, but by 1865 the working arrangement with the GNR had ceased and the S&ER took over the running itself. A disagreement with the LNWR in 1869 as to how much the S&ER should pay for the use of the LNWR station resulted in the junction being closed by the larger company. The outcome was that the S&ER

had to build a temporary wooden platform in a field close to the junction. This terminus was called Sibson and left the poor passengers no choice but to walk through the fields between the two stations. So much for providing a quicker link with London and Peterborough!

The GNR took over the running of the line again in 1872, and very quickly relationships with the LNWR were restored and the junction re-opened in May 1873. The passenger services never exceeded four or five return trips a day, so it is not difficult to see how this branch became an early candidate for closure.

Although the S&ER had remained independent for most of its life, albeit worked by the GNR for many years, it became part of the LNER with the Grouping in 1923. Barnack closed in July 1926, while Ufford Bridge and Wansford Road closed in July 1929. Goods services continued until 1931.

Today Barnack station is a private residence. The platform at Ufford Bridge is still in situ, while at Stamford the station was converted into a private residence in the 1960s and the substantial stone-built goods shed became flats in 1988. Thankfully the town still has the old MR line to provide it with through services between Birmingham, Leicester, Peterborough and Stansted Airport.

Railway preservation centres, museums and other railways in the county

This chapter, which does not claim to be a comprehensive list, covers nine sites in the county, two of which are long closed but are included for historical and interest purposes.

Blakesley Hall Miniature Railway

Blakesley Hall itself dates from 1216, though sadly it was demolished in 1957. In 1876 it became the home of C. W. Bartholomew and his family. He was interested in cars and railways, and this latter interest led him to build a model railway for his son. The next logical step was to build one for himself – obviously the bug had bitten hard! In 1903 he had a 15-inch circular track laid around the grounds of the Hall, with a quarter-mile-long track that ran to Blakesley station on what was then the East & West Junction Railway. At Blakesley a bay platform, parallel with the westbound platform, allowed for easy transfer of passengers.

Initially the motive power consisted of two American Cagney locomotives, but in 1909 Mr Bartholomew wanted to see if it was possible to build a locomotive using a petrol engine. He approached Bassett-Lowke of Northampton, which in turn asked Mr Henry Greenly to design such a locomotive. The result was a 4-4-4 tank engine, powered by a 14hp car engine with a gearbox built by another famous county name, Charles Wicksteed of Kettering. By all accounts it worked well, with speeds up to 32mph being recorded – for a 15-inch system that was quite a speed! The new locomotive was named *Blacolvesley*, which, it is believed, was one of the original spellings of Blakesley. Mr Bartholomew died in 1919, but his widow continued to run the trains until the outbreak of war in 1939, when the whole system was sold to an estate in Yorkshire. *Blacolvesley*, it is believed, has survived and runs occasionally on the Ravenglass & Eskdale Railway in Cumbria.

A postcard view of Alec Wyatt, Bartholomew's engineer, on the Blakesley Hall estate with the carriages he helped to modify from some American stock. The loco is the 4-4-4T *Blacolvesley*. *Author's collection*

Overstone Solarium Light Railway

Of all the railways in this chapter, this is perhaps the least known of them all, due in no small part to the fact that so little was written about it during its short life. Initially it appears to have been the idea of three Bedfordshire men, to create a small working preservation centre for 'anything connected with railways'. There were two short lengths of track, one of 2-foot gauge and the other of standard gauge. The narrow gauge loco was a Hunslet-built 0-4-0T, No 1, dating from 1922 and originating from a North Wales quarry. The standard gauge loco, an 0-6-0, was built by Bagnall and came to Overstone from Cranford. The railway opened to the public in May 1969.

It was claimed that the system could carry up to 1,000 passengers a day at a fare of 2 shillings (10p) for adults and 1 shilling for children. I was fortunate in being part of a group who visited the line in June 1970 and was able to see the narrow gauge loco in steam. By October of that year the standard gauge track had been lifted, and how much longer the remaining track and stock survived

A June 1970 poster advertising the Overstone Solarium Light Railway. *Author's collection*

is not known. Its one claim to fame is that it must have been one of the shortest-lived preservation systems in the county, if not the country.

The 2-foot-gauge Hunslet-built No 1 in steam in June 1970. *Author*

Daventry Garden Railway

I have included this delightful garden railway because of its uniqueness and for the fact that it does have open days, though sadly no one will ever be able to have a ride on it. The railway dates from 1966 when the owner, feeling cramped with his indoor layout, decided to venture outdoors. The use of OO gauge outdoors was practically unknown at the time and the owner encountered many problems, one of which was the fact that the layout was to be built in a smallish sloping garden. On my first visit in 1980 I found a beautifully designed layout that ran with few hiccups and employed a variety of motive power and rolling-stock. In 1997 the decision was taken to change the gauge to Garden (G). At the present time the system has a very American atmosphere, with some impressive American locomotives complete with authentic sound effects. Use of the larger gauge allows the use of steam locomotives, all radio-controlled. Although the number of visitors at any one time is limited, it is well worth the effort. To find out when the open days are, and for further details, contact Mr Burchell on 01327 704135.

Above **The Daventry Garden Railway in its OO-gauge days, May 1980.** *Author*

Left **This realistic scene from August 2005 shows part of the Daventry Garden Railway since its conversion to 'G' gauge.** *Author*

Northamptonshire Ironstone Railway Trust

The railway is based at Hunsbury Hill in Northampton. Two thousand years earlier the Danes had chosen this site, partly because of its position – it is on a hill so was easy to defend – but also because they found deposits of iron ore, which they knew how to use. With the Industrial Revolution requiring increasing amounts of iron ore, the area started to be quarried again, with the iron ore going down the hillside in wagons by gravity and the empty wagons being pulled back up by horses. At the present time the entire area is owned by Northampton Council, and it was in the area of the Danes Camp and the old quarries that it was decided to create a working museum that would focus on the ironstone industry of the county.

A small group of enthusiasts formed the Rushden Railway Society in 1971 and acquired Peckett 0-6-0 metre-gauge locomotive No 87, formerly owned by

The Hunsbury Hill Railway in April 2006, with a platform being constructed near the entrance to the site. *Author*

Stewart & Lloyds at one of the company's quarries in Finedon. In 1974 the Trust was set up formally with grants made available by the Northampton Development Corporation.

In the early days the plan was to have three gauges at Hunsbury: standard, metre and narrow (2 feet). This, it was felt, would represent the widest range used throughout the industry. Subsequently this idea was dropped and it was decided to concentrate only on standard gauge. By 1981 the Trust was calling for more volunteers in order to complete the track-laying and thus qualify for further grants. In the following years a museum has been built, together with a compound to house the rolling-stock. The line was able to start giving rides to the public, but increasing safety concerns led to the line being closed in 2002. Major reconstruction work brought the hope that the line would be re-opened in September 2005, but when I called at the museum at Easter 2006 I found the site closed and with no indication as to when the museum was open to the public.

In 1993 No 87 was transferred, on a long-term basis, to the Irchester Narrow Gauge Railway Trust.

Northampton & Lamport Railway

When the last train ran from Northampton to Market Harborough in August 1981, a group of enthusiasts was already planning to save the branch, or at least part of it. Initially the group called itself the Welland Valley Rail Revival Group, but changed its name in 1983 to Northampton Steam Railway Ltd. Its work concentrated on restoration at Pitsford & Brampton station and the immediate area, the station having closed in June 1950.

Since 1983 work has continued not only at the station but also in extending the line in both directions. During this period it has changed its name again to the Northampton & Lamport Railway. Apart from acquiring

locomotives, rolling-stock and general railway artefacts, the railway has also bought several signal boxes with the intention of bringing them back into service together with the associated manual signalling.

The first passenger-carrying services started in November 1995, with the official opening being held in March of the following year. Thankfully the majority of the trackbed has been retained and converted into a footpath and cycleway, appropriately named the Brampton Valley Way by the County Council. This means that there is room for both railway and footpath to exist together, which will enable the railway to be extended in the future.

Polish 0-6-0ST No 7646 arrives at Pitsford & Brampton station with a down express in March 2005. *Author*

Irchester Narrow Gauge Railway Trust

In the early 1970s a small group who had been involved with the restoration of preserved BR 4-6-2 No 70000 *Britannia* at Bridgnorth decided that they would like to put their expertise to good use, but to do it a little closer to home. The outcome was the decision to buy and restore a locomotive that had worked for many years at a local ironstone quarry. No 85 was a Peckett metre-gauge 0-6-0T locomotive, and at the outset the restoration work started at Hunsbury Hill, but in 1982 the group took a lease from BR on the old goods shed at Irchester. The aim was to purchase the shed, but BR eventually decided not to renew the lease, the consequence being that, after all the work done to restore the shed, never mind the work on the locomotive, the group were about to become homeless. To cut a long story short, they approached the County

Council and suggested that, since the nearby Irchester Country Park was an old ironstone quarry, what better place for a new museum devoted to the railways that worked in the local quarries?

In 1987 the Council signed a 21-year-lease on an area of land within the park. Two years earlier the group had formed the Irchester Narrow Gauge Railway Trust, and realised that if they were going to establish a museum it would require a building. The amount of rolling-stock and artefacts had continued to grow, and the new building would have to be big enough to accommodate all of these and to allow for further acquisitions. In 1987 the building was erected and expansion of the site has continued. A short length of track leads out of the museum compound and runs down part of an original trackbed, which enables demonstrations of the Trust's locomotives.

This museum is unique in the county, and indeed in the country, being devoted solely to metre gauge. With the changing economic and political situation, the Trust is hoping that when its 21-year-lease expires in a few years time, it will be renewed.

Ex-Stewart & Lloyds 0-6-0ST No 85 at the Irchester Narrow Gauge Railway Museum in June 1988. *Author*

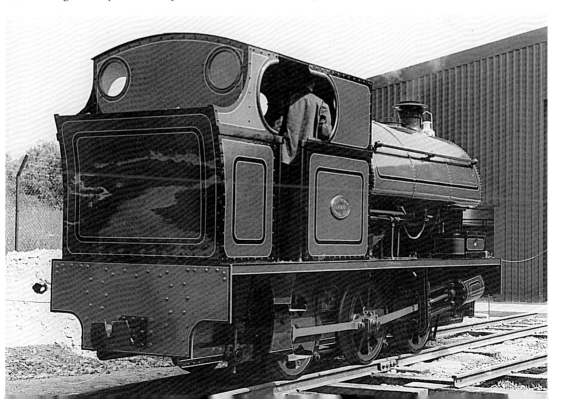

Rushden Historical Transport Trust

After the last goods train on the Higham Ferrers branch ran in November 1969, nothing changed immediately other than the track being lifted. In the mid-1970s the local Council acquired both the station and goods shed at Rushden (the goods shed is still used by the Council). The station was rented out to various businesses, including, rather appropriately, a boot and shoe wholesaler. In 1976 a group of local transport enthusiasts was formed and, realising that they would need somewhere to store and display their collection, approached the Council to see if they could rent the station. The Council

agreed and restoration started. Eventually the Trust was able to buy the entire station site.

Over the intervening years work has continued with track-laying towards Higham Ferrers and the establishment of a museum. One of the waiting rooms at the station has been converted into a bar and has become noted as a centre for real ale. For years the site was threatened by a new road scheme, and although, thankfully, the new road has left the station area intact, it has left the goods shed isolated.

One major acquisition in August 1986 was the disused Midland Railway signal box from East Langton on the Midland Main Line. This is now in the process of being restored to working order.

A pre-preservation view of Rushden station, taken in July 1972. *Author*

The Rushden Historical Transport Trust headquarters with 0-4-0ST *Edmundsons* in the platform and the signal box from East Langton at the platform end in November 2000. *Author*

Wicksteed Park

There are some railway enthusiasts who would claim that this railway should not be included since it is seen only as a 'toy railway for children'. However, I think differently. 2006 will be the 75th anniversary of the line opening, and in its 75 years it has probably carried more children and adults than all the other preserved railways in the county put together!

Wicksteed Park is a well-known pleasure park in Northamptonshire. Charles Wicksteed was born in Leeds in 1847, but established his engineering business in Kettering. He prospered and wanted to do something for the townsfolk. In 1913 he purchased the first area of land for his proposed park, and over the next 15 years he bought more land and

continued to develop the park and all the facilities, including the still popular water chute.

In 1930 Charles Wicksteed wanted to add a new attraction, namely a miniature railway, and work started almost immediately on the 1¼-mile 2-foot-gauge line. The line, which runs round the boating lake with a station in the park, opened to the public in April 1931. The three diesel-engined steam-outline locomotives have been at the park from the line's opening.

History was made in August 2005 when, for the first time, a steam locomotive was used to see how it would cope. *Peter Pan*, an 0-4-0ST, was loaned by the Leighton Buzzard Railway and worked well. It is hoped to repeat this venture in 2006 as part of the 75th anniversary celebrations.

Cheyenne **with a train at the lakeside halt at Wicksteed Park in 1974.**
Author

The first ever steam locomotive to run at Wicksteed Park: *Peter Pan*, **on loan from the Leighton Buzzard Sand Railway, works a trial train in August 2005.** *Author*

Nene Valley Railway

Although this railway is only just in the county, at Yarwell, it has been included for the sake of completeness.

In 1968 the Rev Richard Paten bought from BR for £3,000 Standard 4-6-0 No 73050. The intention was for it to become a static exhibit at Peterborough as a reminder of the long historical links between the city and railways. This move could be said to have been the start of what was to become the Nene Valley Railway. Having acquired the locomotive it was found to be in a better condition than at first thought, and the idea to restore it to working order was born. It was named *City of Peterborough* in August 1972.

The Peterborough Locomotive Society realised that having a working locomotive meant that you needed somewhere to run it. In the early 1970s BR was still running goods traffic to Oundle, and the Society commissioned a feasibility study to see if the section of line between Orton and Wansford could be used; the study indicated that the idea was indeed viable. Meanwhile Peterborough Development Corporation wanted to create a country park in the Orton area, so the Society suggested that the proposed park might include a preserved railway as an added attraction. The Corporation was in agreement and put up the money to buy the stretch of line from BR.

Then a member bought a Swedish locomotive, which had been built to the Continental loading gauge, ie higher and wider than the British standard. The decision was then taken to change all the structures on the line to continental standards.

Early days of what was to become the Nene Valley Railway: BR Standard Class 5 4-6-0 No 73050, named *City of Peterborough*, stands at the British Sugar Corporation's sidings in May 1973. *Author*

The new booking hall/café/shop of the Nene Valley Railway at Wansford, September 1996. *Author*

On a weekend in March 1974 volunteers re-laid the connection between the BR main line and Longville Junction to enable stock to be transferred.

Over the years work has continued, including, in 1995/6, perhaps one of the railway's most ambitious projects. This was the new building complex at Wansford, which contains the booking office, shops, café and offices. More recently there are plans to build a new station with a run-round loop at Yarwell. Since this development is adjacent to an arm of the River Nene, there are also plans to provide trips on the river from proposed new moorings at Yarwell.

INDEX